REACHING FOR HEAVEN

"In this gem of a guide, Michael Amodei offers a thoughtful and practical framework for how we can turn our attention, devotion, and action to God in our post-retirement years. With wit and wisdom, the book offers a template for how reflections of our past, present, and current plans and prayer can serve as a compass on our return journey to God. For those who are intentional about their salvation, this book is a companion."

Carolyn Woo
Distinguished President's Fellow for Global Development, Purdue University
Former President and Chief Executive Officer, Catholic Relief Services

"Mike Amodei and I are together on the field for every Notre Dame football game as he's the field supervisor of ushers and I'm the team chaplain. We both agree it's a piece of heaven, and our conversations are often edifying and spirit-filled. In this book, Amodei shares some deeply practical ways to truly prepare for eternal life from things we might already know but can all improve upon: praying, friendship, empathizing with the poor, and devoting ourselves to Mary."

Fr. Nate Wills, CSC
The Mary Ann Remick Leadership Program, Alliance for Catholic Education
University of Notre Dame Football Chaplain

"Knowing him for almost half his life, I know that Mike Amodei loves God, his Church, and Notre Dame (I'm pretty sure in that order!). In this easy-to-read book, Amodei shares his own experiences and reflections on the relationships that have shaped his life as he prepares to enter retirement. His insights and suggestions will spur the thoughts and commitments of Catholics wishing to make the final stages of their earthly journey the most meaningful."

Mary Elizabeth Sperry
Author of *Making Room for God: Decluttering and the Spiritual Life*

"Happiness is not about getting what you want but being content with what you have. Based on my personal experience, if you follow these suggestions—attend Mass daily, serve the poor, make a pilgrimage, and reconnect with friends—you will have a happy life. I have known Mike Amodei for the past twenty-plus years, and I do not know a finer Catholic who cares more about people and the future of this country. If you buy this book, read it, and put your faith in Our Lady, miracles can happen."

Lou Holtz
Former University of Notre Dame Football Coach
Author of the bestselling *The Fighting Spirit* and *A Teen's Game Plan for Life*

"When I was in my forties, I ran a ten-mile race and was feeling pretty good about running seven-minute miles until we approached the finish line and I heard the public address announcer congratulating the seventy-eight-year-old runner who finished just ahead of me! At first, I was mortified that I was beaten by someone who was almost an octogenarian. Then I was inspired to keep running well into my senior years. Now in my seventies myself and still running, I draw renewed inspiration from Amodei's new book, *Reaching for Heaven*. Sharing an abundance of personal experiences, Amodei makes the stories of the Bible and teachings of the Church come alive with life lessons to help guide readers into their senior years and beyond, reminding us that our life today is only the beginning as we look forward to the glories of heaven."

Most Reverend Thomas John Paprocki
Bishop of Springfield in Illinois

"As a long-time friend and parishioner at St. Monica, Mike Amodei has spent most of his life in faithful service to God and the Church. This book is a testimony of someone who spent more than thirty years in adult faith formation. Amodei combines humor with wisdom to show you how to face your golden years with confidence and hope."

Msgr. Lloyd Torgerson
Pastor of St. Monica Catholic Community in Santa Monica, California

REACHING FOR HEAVEN

14
Spiritual Goals
as You
Grow Older

MICHAEL AMODEI

AVE MARIA PRESS AVE Notre Dame, Indiana

Founded in 1865, Ave Maria Press is a ministry of the United States Province of Holy Cross.

www.avemariapress.com

Paperback: ISBN-13 978-1-64680-274-6

E-book: ISBN-13 978-1-64680-275-3

Cover image © gettyimages.com.

Cover design by Kristen Hornyak Bonelli.

Text design by Christopher D. Tobin.

Printed and bound in the United States of America.

Library of Congress Cataloging-in-Publication Data is available.

JMJ

+

CONTENTS

INTRODUCTION
Getting Ready for My Judgment Day

When you look back on your life, what are some of the things you'd still like to accomplish? Are you harboring any regrets—or any unfulfilled dreams?

I missed out on the heyday of Fulton J. Sheen. In the early 1950s, he had a prime-time television show, *Life Is Worth Living*, that aired on Tuesday nights at 8 p.m. The Catholic bishop (who would eventually be an archbishop), unpaid for his efforts, stood in front of a blackboard on which he scribbled the letters JMJ for Jesus, Mary, and Joseph, and gave talks without a script or cue cards on various religious themes. The program was so popular that it even occasionally garnered higher ratings than the well-known and promoted *Milton Berle Show*. Berle commented, "If I'm going to be eased off the top by anyone, it's better that I lose to the One for whom Bishop Sheen is speaking."[1]

My uncle Bill and my grandmother kept up with Archbishop Sheen after his show went off the air, so I heard of him when I was a kid. Nowadays I sometimes watch *Life Is Worth Living* on YouTube or listen to his sermons on Spotify. I have a feeling that because Archbishop Sheen was so media savvy in his time, he would not be surprised to know he has fans using these mediums and tuning in to him in the twenty-first century.

Sheen talked often about death and judgment: "A happy death is a masterpiece, and no masterpiece was ever perfected in a day. Death is a beautiful thing for those who die before they die, by dying to the daily temptations of the world, the flesh, and the devil."² Sheen explained that what the Church calls our particular judgment with Christ himself, which will occur right after our death, will be "an evaluation of ourselves as we really are." He added, "Your works follow you."³

Sheen's television show was broadcast live before a studio audience at the Adelphi Theatre in New York. There were no do-overs. It's amazing that he was so good at it. Our particular judgment doesn't have any do-overs either. "Do not think when you go before the judgment seat of God that you will argue a case. Do not think that you will be your own jury," Sheen said. In other words, our actions in this life will speak for themselves.⁴

As Catholics, we know that each of us at the end of life will be asked to give account for how we spent our time here on earth. And since none of us knows how much time we have left, we need to do the important things today.

Imagine you are standing before Christ right now, at the moment of death. For what will you apologize, and for what will you be most thankful? Are there ways you would like to be more intentional about how you practice the faith?

This book is a kind of wake-up call, a chance to become a better Catholic—so that when we face that one-on-one with Jesus, we don't have to fear what is coming.

WHAT GOALS DO YOU HAVE?

What do you have in mind now? Do you still have goals and want to be productive? I know I do. I'm a baby boomer who still has a few dreams and goals left. I would like to continue to see how much I can accomplish before I die. I also want to spend a focused amount of time reviewing my life so I can both apologize for where I have failed and be thankful for all I have been given. There's no way to know how many years I have left, so I want to do these important things today. I also want to do some more involved things in the near future that I haven't had a chance to do in the past. Older age does seem to afford us more time.

With that being said, I want to be more intentional about being a better Catholic and disciple of Jesus Christ. I can't believe how cavalier and unintentional I have been about what is coming. This meeting with Christ at the very moment of death will decide whether I will proceed directly to the blessedness of heaven, or to heaven after first being purified in purgatory, or immediately to hell and eternal damnation. I, and you probably as well, take some comfort with my faith in Christ, the Just Judge, who I know loves me and is filled with mercy. Even so, I want to put my best foot forward by preparing for that meeting with less trepidation and more excitement because I will be face-to-face with my Lord and I want to revel in the experience, not cower in it.

In school, we had tests. Sometimes we were happy just to pass. If we failed a test, we usually got a chance to make it up. This test on Judgment Day has no do-overs. I don't want a barely passing grade either. I want a plan that focuses on passing that test with flying colors and getting to heaven. I want Jesus to tell me "job well done." This is a book for Catholics who want that too. The ideas presented here are to offer you encouragement to look back at your own life and formulate your own concrete plans for ways you can be a more intentional and better Catholic. The risks are few. The rewards are great.

COMING TO FAITH

First, let's start out from where you are right now: You're a good person. You love your family. You believe in God. You practice your Catholic faith (or are preparing to be received into the Church), but you think you can do even better if you had more time. This is the place where I find myself at least. I'm also well aware I'm deep into the second half of life.

In any case, if you're anything like me, your knowledge of God and the truths of the Church came via a circuitous route. For me, this has a lot to do with growing up when I did and the state of the Church during my formative years.

Let me explain.

I started first grade in September 1963, the same month that the new pope, Paul VI, reconvened the Second Vatican Council. Did those in charge imagine that the kids my age would really be the pilot audience for what was going on in Rome? We were immediately the test case.

I went to CCD on Saturday mornings at our parish, St. Luke's Church in Temple City, California, a suburban town fifteen miles east of downtown Los Angeles and, at the time, right out of the Mayberry set of *The Andy Griffith Show*. Because my first grade of CCD occurred before the council had taken any hold, we learned questions and answers that made us think about God being everywhere and knowing all things, heard stories about Jesus who walked on water and healed blind people, and sang songs to his Mother and put a crown on her head.

When I started second grade, the first vestiges of change were sweeping the Church, and the curriculum changed. Instead of hearing Bible stories, we made collages with butterflies to represent new life and covered shoeboxes with crepe paper and pasted photos we cut from *National Geographic* and *LIFE* magazines on them to represent, well, I'm still not sure.

I finished out CCD through Confirmation in seventh grade. By that year, 1970, I don't remember much of what was taught or shared or whether we had a book to read. I do remember my Stingray bike was missing one night after class ended. Fr. Blaire, who became a bishop, turned on the floodlights in the church parking lot, and we found it ditched in the side alley next to the rectory. That is my last memory of religious education.

Throughout my years in public high school, I went to the 5:30 Sunday Mass by myself, where I would stand in the back of the church and talk with my friends. I did continue to pray, mostly that my parents would not get sick and die, but I wasn't sure where my prayers were headed or who the God was who was listening. In this part of my life, I was truly living the words on the "Footsteps in the Sand" poster. Remember the poem by Margaret Fishback Powers, in which she envisions life to be like a beach, with a set of footprints in the sand that belong to Jesus, who carries us through the tough times?

My life was a bit like that: I saw one set of footprints and figured they belonged to me alone. The truth was, Jesus was carrying me . . . and waiting just for the right moment when I might be interested in actually knowing him. For me, that moment came at the baccalaureate Mass just before my college graduation at Loyola Marymount University. I remember praying, "God, are you real? If so, let me know." This kind of prayer turns out to be right up God's alley, and he answered it posthaste.

FINDING GOD

In the fall of 1979, after my graduation, I coached the fifth-grade Catholic Youth Organization (CYO) basketball team at St. Monica's, a parish and school near the Pacific Ocean in Santa Monica. This wasn't my dream job; I was doing it only until I could lock in on something better. I also had to move back home after living on my own at college. I think there were hostages in Iran and the Moscow Olympics were already being boycotted by this time. The world seemed a mess, and I wasn't feeling all that great either.

Our team was playing a game on a windy afternoon outside on the asphalt court. We had seven players. Six of them were pretty good, and the other was Kenny Waller. Kenny wore Hush Puppies and black socks with his uniform. He was about four foot five and seventy-five pounds, with hair that fell nearly to his shoulders. His ragged St. Monica Falcon uniform shorts had little elastic, and they periodically dipped to his knees as he ran up and down the asphalt court, holding up his shorts with clenched fists.

As Kenny passed the center line, I noticed Sandra Valdivia, another fifth grader, turning the numbers on one of those flip-chart scoreboards on the sideline. She had two skinned knees and a dirty, sweaty face from playing with the boys during our team warmups. She was a better player than Kenny Waller and

xvi   Reaching for Heaven

maybe a couple of the other boys too, but she couldn't play in the game because she was a girl.

So, Sandra sat on the sideline, occasionally fending off Earl Moosbruger, a kid from her class, with punches and kicks. Earl kept giving her a hard time because he wanted to steal her job as scorekeeper. Because it was windy, the flip-chart numbers wouldn't stick and the score kept getting all messed up. The boys on our team kept yelling at Sandra, "FIX THE SCORE!" Sandra would yell back at them. One time, she also gave them the middle finger.

I was really taking all of this in. Wind. Cold. Kenny holding up his shorts. Sandra punching Earl. Score not sticking. Ah hah! This was beautiful! The canceled Olympics and hostages and no real job didn't matter. There had to be a God who had created such a scene! There had to be a good God who made Kenny and Sandra and Earl. This game, and my time at St. Monica's School coaching the team in general, was the real start of my belief.

THREE GOSPEL PASSAGES AND A LITTLE BOOK

What happens with awakened faith? We begin to pay attention to other similar ways God is present. Prayer and sacraments take on new meanings as we engage them with greater conviction. We begin to read the Bible with new attention and vigor. Certain scripture passages become ingrained in our thoughts and form our goals and motivations. This is what happened with me. Three gospel passages in particular stood out for me as I began to plan this next part of life. I share them with you here; maybe they can inspire you too, or remind you of other particular scripture passages that do.

1. "Can any of you by worrying add a single moment to your life-span?" (Mt 6:27)

For those of us in the baby boomer generation, it is almost impossible not to be plagued by some worry and anxiety. First, there were the pressures of many years of school, jumping into society in the eighties, finding a place to live, and paying for expenses after college. But on a deeper level, we had other worries as we came of age back then. We witnessed childhood friends sink into drug abuse. Divorce was more prevalent. My sister's marriage ended, and my sweet niece faced life in a single-parent household, something our family wasn't used to.

As we got older, death began to lurk. The twenty-four-year-old brother of a good friend discovered a mole between his toes one June. He died five months later from Stage IV melanoma. I wasn't naive enough to not know that I was one errant driver in an intersection away from my own death.

Jesus's question and the entirety of the passage in Matthew 6:25–34 were right in my face. I remember sharing it with my mom, who lived with more anxiety than even I did. The birds don't worry about what the day will bring. God provides for the birds. The flowers don't stress about how they appear to others. Nothing is more beautiful than the colorful wildflowers. "Are not you more important than they?" (Mt 6:26b). God does know our needs. God loves us more than the birds. We only need to trust God.

2. "Take my yoke upon you and learn from me, for I am meek and humble of heart; and you will find rest for yourselves" (Mt 11:29)

This "yoke," this crosspiece that work animals bore upon their backs, resembles the cross Jesus carried on his own back. It also resembles the physical strains we face in our own lives.

Being human comes with pain. There are not many who reach their sixties without some chronic pain or haven't already faced battles with heart disease, diabetes, cancer, and more. I don't expect these years between the midsixties and death to be pain free. Recently, I had cataract surgery. Not really a major procedure in the medical scheme of things. But as I was laying in the bed, gown on, staring at the hospital ceiling, I had a thought:

There was a decent chance that this particular experience of prepping for a procedure, laying in a hospital bed with a funny gown on, was but a preview of what might come in the next decade or so. Reality, right?

But when we carry these physical pains with purpose, the mental burden *is* light. I learned that lesson naturally at other times in my life. As a kid, I trained for sports. The practice and exercise were exhausting and physically taxing. The rewards of being on the team and playing in the games were great. Nowadays, the nearly three hours I spend on Saturdays trimming the bushes and cutting the lawn leave me nearly crippled for the rest of the evening. But when I'm done, I sit on the back porch admiring the manicured yard while sipping a cold drink from a bottle. In the big picture of life and death, Jesus makes the hard stuff worth it, not just for the reward that comes when we are finished but also for the deep inner satisfaction we get while we are carrying the painful yoke for him.

3. *"Remain in my love. . . . I have told you this so that my joy may be in you and your joy may be complete" (Jn 15:9b, 11)*

Because of my age (I was under the age of twelve in 1960s Southern California), I was not *directly* affected by Vietnam or the culture shifts of the decade; as a teenager in the "Me Generation" of the 1970s, I have known plenty of temporal joy and freedom.

Compared to those who lived in other times and places, my life has been carefree and happy. When you grow up with an inequitable helping of goodness, it's hard not to want this to continue. I still want the same sense of freedom I had when my best friend Jon Halladay and I would take off on our bikes at age ten and be gone from early morning to dusk. I want a life with the same kind of friendship we had as teenagers when a group of us guys and girls spent the day on the sand sunning ourselves at the beach. I want a life with the kind of joy that came with meeting and dating my wife Lisa and getting married at the church and partying hard in the parish hall afterward.

My life has been a blessing in every way, and I don't want to see those blessings slip through my fingers. And why should they? Our God is a good God. Pain is in the world, yes. But there is so much love, so much joy. You may think of these things differently than I do. But I'm guessing that perfect love and joy, as promised by Jesus, are what we are all after.

Around the time I first began to recognize how God was acting in my life, I also picked up a little book called *Abundonment to Divine Providence* by a Jesuit, Jean-Pierre de Caussade, written in the eighteenth century. The message seemed at once very difficult to me, yet absolutely simple: God is always acting in our daily lives. In *everyone's* daily life and in *every* second of our day. If we look closely, we see God and we find meaning. This might be in things such as recognizing how the rainy day that caused you to miss your outdoor plans led you to do something productive indoors instead. It might be in the harsh words spoken to you that you might brush off and ignore at first but have deeper meaning upon reflection. Everything comes from God. "Even all the hairs of your head are counted" (Mt 10:30).

Peace comes from abandoning ourselves to his divine will. Further on in life, I recognized that God allows the Holy Spirit to dispense the graces of his will through the actions of his Mother, Mary. And yet, as much as I wanted to follow the advice of de Caussade and at least attempt to notice how God was speaking to me in the present moments of each day, I'm not saintly enough to practice these things at all times. One thing the strategy of abandonment did lead me to do was also look back in my life for very obvious times when God was trying to say something to me when I wasn't paying attention. "Looking back" is a key part of any plan that looks ahead.

LOOK BACK IN GRATITUDE; LOOK AHEAD WITH HOPE

Only in looking back with gratitude at our life does the future ahead of us look bright, giving us confidence that God will continue to be faithful as he has in the past. Our past gives us many keys to what's coming. In explaining his famous Daily Examen, a prayerful daily reflection we can offer to detect God's presence in our lives and to discern our future direction, St. Ignatius Loyola said that "the first point is to give thanks to God our Lord for the gifts received."[5] Our first action should always be gratitude. Every breath we take is a gift. Do you think a person finally taken off a ventilator post-surgery might agree?

By looking back with a spirit of gratitude, it is easier to imagine what eternal life will be—for recognizing how God acted in our past will make us more comfortable about how he will act with us in the future. "What eye has not seen, and ear has not heard, and what has not entered the human heart, what God has prepared for those who love him," writes St. Paul to the Corinthians (1 Cor 2:9).

Pope Francis also spoke of the need for us to look back at our memories and see not only the beautiful things God has done for us but also the obstacles that have been placed in our way and the times we have missed God's benevolent actions in our lives because of our own sinfulness:

> It is good for the Christian heart to memorize our journey, our personal journey: just like the Lord who accompanied us up here and held us by the hand. And the times I said to our Lord: "No! Go away! I don't want you!" Our Lord respects our wishes. But we must memorize our past and be a memorial of our own lives and our own journey. We must look back and remember and do it often. "At that time God gave me this grace and I replied in that way, I did this or that . . . he accompanied me." And in this way we arrive at a new encounter, an encounter of gratitude.[6]

Taking stock of our past is also useful in showing us how we can still be of service in this life, though perhaps in different ways and with greater intentionality. In the past, I coached a CYO basketball team in Santa Monica, California, as a young kid with no teaching or coaching experience. Now, with the benefits of experience, I could help administer a sports league for kids or mentor parents who are coaching their kids in sports for the first time.

The experiences of the past can point to future goals in the spiritual life too. Over the course of my life, I have gone to Mass every Sunday and sometimes on Fridays. In the future, I would like to be a daily Mass-goer. In the past, I was angry with my neighbor who ran into my car and didn't cover the damages. In the future, I would like to bury that incident and be cordial with him. In the past, I took my children to Mass and talked to them about God so they would grow up to be faithful Catholics. Now I want to pray for them and be a better example of my own faith.

There are a lot of other productive things we might want to do as time passes. None of them really involve reinventing the wheel. They are based on experiences we have already had and ways we have been close with God in the past—or making amends for things we regret, such as ignoring God, being unkind to our neighbor, or other sinful choices. No matter how old you are, you can set goals and aspirations that will make your remaining time on earth full of purpose and meaning, so you can face the future with confidence and hope.

But what if you set these goals for yourself and aren't able to follow through? There are ways to adapt your goals and get them started and finished in a shorter time frame.

YOU PLAN, GOD LAUGHS

An old Yiddish proverb goes like this: "If you want to make God laugh, tell him your plans." Life is full of little surprises, some more welcome than others: Send the "last" kid off to school, and find out you will be welcoming a surprise addition in nine months or so. Save up for a vacation; the dryer goes out, and you need a new one. Make a ten-year plan with your spouse, and death pays a visit.

Jesus told a parable with a similar message. A man builds larger barns to store all his grains and extra goods so he can spend the rest of his life resting, eating, drinking, and being merry. Then God tells him he will be dead that very night. God also calls him a fool. We can take one part of this "parable of the rich fool" to heart: at any time of life—and especially at age sixty-four and beyond—our plans are subject to change.

You ever watch an offensive coordinator of a football team close up? (I actually have. I've been on the Notre Dame football sidelines since 1996 as "field supervisor" for ushers, a great gig!) The coordinator comes out with a huge cardboard sheet with twenty or so plays scripted that he wants the team to run in order to begin the game. Sometimes the plan works to perfection and the team gets through all twenty plays and scores two or three touchdowns. But other times the opposing defensive coach has anticipated what is on the play card and throws a wrench in the plans. The offensive coach has to come up with something else, fast, and when he does the scripted play card gets discarded on the ground (and then put in the trash bin by the field supervisor).

In making our own plans, we are like that football coach (or that rich fool), experiencing a change of plans at the drop of a hat. That doesn't mean we can't make plans—we can and should have some productive things in mind to do over the next number of years. However, we should also have a backup plan in place.

For example, is there something on your list intended for some time off in the future that, with adjustments, you can begin to do now? For example, while I am researching ways to set up a youth sports program for underserved kids, I will also volunteer to help coach a team in a program already in place. While I would love to go to 7 a.m. daily Mass, until I don't have a job to go to and a son to drive to work, I'll figure out how to add one midday Mass to my weekly schedule. This book will contain ideas for both larger and longer-term plans and more condensed and immediate plans.

Above all, we don't want to be like the rich fool in Jesus's parable, storing up property for selfish reasons. If we want to end up on the right side of eternity, it's important to practice unselfishness and to make plans that incorporate prayer, service, reconciliation, relationship-building, studying, and cross-carrying with a spirit of gratitude. There will be no selfishness or foolishness in our motivations. Or at least we will limit them as much as possible.

CREATING A PLAN FOR LIFE

In the Catholic tradition, a "plan for life" might be called different things: a "rule of life," "plan for spiritual growth," or "spiritual direction" to name just three. These spiritual plans all have the same important end-goal: growing in love and virtue so that, by God's grace, we can reach heaven. Effective plans will include daily prayer, acts of consecration, attending Mass, spiritual reading, devotions to Mary and the saints, reflection, frequent sacramental confession, civility and kindness, and practicing the virtues—all done while giving thanks.

The plan for life outlined in this book draws on each of these spiritual practices and offers practical ways to incorporate them into meaningful experiences. Remember, we want our years ahead prior to death to be ones of productivity; we want to be as active as possible. To do so will require thinking about the things we want to do; planning how, when, and where we want to do them; and then getting out and putting them into practice. Time is always limited, no matter how old you are. Some things we will do before death will be hard. Reconciling with the guy down the street who drove into my car comes to mind. Other things will not be of our choosing. I don't want to get sick, but that may happen, and if it does, I want to make the most of it.

Make sure your plan is adaptable, able to accommodate sudden changes in your situation. Every age has variables that can get in the way of a plan; older ages seem to have even more. The important thing is to start now. This book also offers simple suggestions for enacting a version of each experience. I have drawn on my own memories and with my own plans in mind, but with the additional hope that my descriptions will spur your own memories and plans.

While you may choose to read from start to finish without interruption, I suggest that you read one experience at a time and then pause to allow it to resonate with your own life. For example, you might read one experience per day or every other day. You might also read one experience as part of a Holy Hour devotion. Use the pray and reflect items as a starting point to keep a journal to record (1) personal memories, (2) a dream list for future plans, and (3) ways to begin to practice a facsimile of the experience today.

You might even work through these experiences with your spouse or with a group of fellow pilgriming Catholics. The experiences can be read and shared with several different groups including, but not limited to, RCIA, men's and women's groups, prayer groups, and parent groups. Group members should read an assigned experience before meetings. Plan to share with your group in a discussion format your own personal memories, future plans, and ways to practice the experience today. Use the reflection items as discussion starters. Conclude each session with prayer.

Each chapter is organized in the same way. After a short introduction that names one main experience and its objectives, there are the following sections:

Remember the Past

How is this experience part of your memory? What are some times and ways you have already done what you are planning to do? What can you learn from your memories?

Plan for the Future

What are ways you can enact this experience in the future? Where are opportunities to participate with those already doing the same thing you want to do? What do you hope to gain from the experience? What will be the challenges to complete this goal? What spiritual reward do you hope to gain from the experience? When do you want to do this experience?

Act in the Present

How can you practice for the experience by doing something now? How can you do a condensed version of the experience?

Pray and Reflect

Each chapter ends with a short prayer and three points for personal reflection.

We don't know each other by name. Our age and life experiences may be different. One of us may have experienced more joy or suffering than the other, or grew up having lots of possessions or having fewer. Don't be afraid to adapt these ideas to fit your own particular circumstances. Regardless of our unique circumstances, we share in the gift of being born. We also share in the promise of eternity. I hope to meet you all when we have arrived in heaven. I will be thankful.

> For who can know God's counsel,
>   or who can conceive what the Lord intends?
> For the deliberations of mortals are timid,
>   and uncertain are our plans.
> For the corruptible body burdens the soul
>   and the earthly tent weighs down the mind with
>   its many concerns.

Scarcely can we guess the things on earth,
　　and only with difficulty grasp what is at hand;
　　but things in heaven, who can search them out?
Or who can know your counsel, unless you give
　　Wisdom and send your holy spirit from on high?
Thus were the paths of those on earth made straight.
　　　　　　　　　　　　　　—Wisdom 9:13–18a

1

DISCOVER WHO YOU REALLY ARE

As we begin this phase of life, a self-examination is important. We ask the basic big questions with more urgency: Why am I here? What is the purpose of my life? And what legacy will I leave behind? Christian tradition suggests we take on a trusted and holy person as a partner to help us know more about ourselves and how God acts in our lives. This is known as spiritual direction.

As we continue this process of self-examination, we can also greatly benefit from the opportunity to confess our sins and cleanse our souls in the Sacrament of Reconciliation. In this sacrament we have a chance to return to the purity of the occasion of our Baptism and to begin to glimpse the life God intended for us before we were even conceived.

REMEMBER THE PAST

I don't mean to start chapter 1 out on a downer, but if we are really going to have a chance for eternal life with the Father, Jesus, Mary, the saints, family, and friends, we do need to bring up a topic most of us would rather avoid: the reality of sin. Even if we try to avoid the moral relativism that is so prevalent today, it's easy to buy in to the thought that since we have for the most part lived a moral life, God will excuse us from what we have done and what we have failed to do, outside of major things like theft, murder, and adultery. But is this really so?

The *Catechism of the Catholic Church* teaches that if mortal sin (the name for a grave sin) "is not redeemed by repentance and God's forgiveness, it causes exclusion from Christ's kingdom and the eternal death of hell" (1861). This is kind of like reading the fine print of a car loan. We do need to be aware of mortal sin and its dangers.

If the purpose of the Christian life is to become the most authentic version of ourselves, and to cultivate virtue, one of the most common forms of grave sin falls in the category of self-deception, of pretending to be someone I am not, out of pride or greed (or one of the other deadly sins).

I've done this at certain times in various stages of life. I was a shy kid around girls in high school. As my buddies easily made the transition to going on dates and sharing comfortable conversations with girls, I stayed at home Saturday nights watching *All in the Family* and *The Mary Tyler Moore Show*. When I went away to college, I decided to reinvent myself and imitate exactly how my high school friends behaved around girls. I would be loud, tell big stories, and do daring things. Once I jumped on the stage of a campus movie theater and told the audience the movies had been cancelled. (They hadn't.) Another time, while taking a date home to her dorm after a party, I drove across a manicured lawn and spun doughnuts with my car. (That was our only date.)

I had a new edge to my personality and found that getting into the character of my high school friends allowed me to be comfortable with meeting and talking to girls. What I forgot was that Monica Rodriguez, someone who knew me from my hometown, also went to my college. I would sometimes give her rides home on the weekend. On one of the drives, she said bluntly, "Do you know I liked you better before when you were more thoughtful and polite? You didn't need to change who you are." It was a zinger that kind of stuck.

As I got older, I tried my best to answer the repeated questions of the band of the same name: "Who are you? Who, who, who, who?" Was I the reflective person who prayed out of the Bible and read Thomas Merton during the week before falling asleep, or the guy who swore loudly and listened to off-base jokes with his guy friends and, despite Monica's warning, was still too loud and obnoxious with girls on weekends? At a certain point I realized it would be better to be consistent and put my best and most honest foot forward at all times. The process took some soul searching . . . and a fair amount of time in the confessional.

Really, at the time, I wanted to be more like Rocky Dennis. Do you recognize the name? They made a movie about Rocky in the eighties called *Mask*. Rocky had an extremely rare skeletal disorder that left his face deformed. Yet Rocky was comfortable in his own skin. He had a loving mother (played by Cher in the movie) and a mixture of friends of his mom and others in the neighborhood who grew up with him and knew the real Rocky and did not judge him on his appearance.

In one memorable scene in the movie, Rocky (played by Eric Stoltz) is in one of those fun house carnival mazes with mirrors that distort a person's appearance. However, with Rocky, the mirror really made his face appear "normal," as if he did not have the skeletal condition. Rocky takes a few seconds to examine what he would look like if he did not have his disease and then bounds back outside where he goes on with the rest of his day and the rest of his life. *The cool thing was, he didn't need to keep going back to the mirror.* He didn't need the "what could have been" to make him comfortable with who he is.

Most of us don't do as well as Rocky. When we get some years on us, we tend to look back on our lives and think how different life could have been if we had made one decision over another. We can usually shrug off the types of regrets that have to do with worldly things like pursuing the wrong major in college or not buying certain real estate property when we had the chance. But when we try to bury or ignore patterns of sin that have taken root inside of us, it's hard to make progress in discovering or rediscovering who we are created to be. It's more like spinning our wheels.

It wasn't long after I decided to reclaim the "real me" that I began to return regularly to the Sacrament of Reconciliation. While the format of the sacrament had changed a bit from when I was a kid, the clear resolve in the voice of the priest who offered absolution on behalf of God and the Church still brought with it a feeling that my insides had been cleansed. Going to Confession wasn't a therapy session; it was a chance to acknowledge the wrong I had done and start over on the right path.

When I meet Jesus, I want to meet him as the person I was meant to be. I don't want to be acting. I don't want to be fake. I want to be the person who screams out the window when my team (Dodgers or White Sox) hits a home run and I am listening to the game in the car. I want to be the person who shares a morning conversation with my wife. She definitely knows the real me. I want to be the person who falls asleep at night listening to a scripture reading or a reflective prayer on Spotify. And I want to be the person who comes bounding out of church on Saturday morning after going to Confession feeling spotless and clean.

PLAN FOR THE FUTURE

God's words to the prophet Jeremiah are meant for all of us: "Before I formed you in the womb I knew you" (Jer 1:5a). Before my life is over, I really want to know two things: what God thought of me when he created me and what he thinks of me now.

The Creator put time and thought into making each of us. Our DNA is unique among all people who have ever lived. He must have had something equally unique in mind for us besides our physical makeup. I want to know God the Creator better so that I can know myself the created in a way that I should.

One way to come to a better understanding of these things is through spiritual direction. The practice of spiritual direction was once something done only by monks, nuns, and other mystics. But since the Second Vatican Council, spiritual direction has become increasingly popular among lay Catholics, a way God uses other people to guide us to him.

Spiritual direction is rooted in scripture. On the road from Jerusalem to Gaza, the apostle Philip encountered an Ethiopian man sitting in his chariot reading from the book of Isaiah. Motivated by the Holy Spirit, Philip caught up with the man and said to him, "'Do you understand what you are reading?' He replied, 'How can I, unless someone instructs me?'" (Acts 8:30–31). The rest of the passage talks about Philip instructing the man about the reading, proclaiming Jesus to him, and eventually baptizing him when they came upon water near the road. Can you imagine the missed opportunity if Philip had not been there to direct the man toward God?

You probably have some sense of being spiritually directed at various times, especially when making important decisions. When I was about to move my family across country from California to Indiana, I was torn about leaving my parents, sister, niece, and friends behind. For this move I really needed the advice of someone I trusted.

I decided to talk to my parish priest. "How do I know if this is what God wants for me and my family?" I asked him. He told me that, because he knew me, he knew the job I was heading to would be fulfilling for me and in line with what I had always wanted to do. "But what about my family?" I went on, meaning my larger family, including my parents. "The only family you need to be responsible for are your wife and your own children," he said. The advice was clear and direct. It was what I needed to hear. I accepted the job the next day.

What is spiritual direction? Spiritual direction resembles Philip's encounter with the Ethiopian and my seeking advice from my parish priest, though more regular and intentional. In spiritual direction, you rely on someone "more advanced" in knowledge about God and, perhaps, what it means to grow in holiness. How does this happen? Basically, it occurs in one-to-one meetings in which a spiritual director leaves plenty of room for God to have his voice heard.

Actually, the name spiritual *director* is a misnomer. A spiritual director listens to the directee and then makes *suggestions* that build on the discoveries the person seems on the brink of about himself or herself or about God. For example, if the person seems focused on questioning the redemptive meaning of suffering, the director may suggest scripture passages and other readings that seem apropos. Or if the person has already been doing spiritual reading on this topic, the spiritual director may suggest journaling prompts to help him or her go deeper and more prayerfully into this line of thought.

It's important to know what spiritual direction is not. It is not Confession. The Sacrament of Reconciliation is for naming sins (without much detail really) and receiving absolution. Spiritual direction is also not a self-improvement program, psychological counseling, or self-therapy. These worthy endeavors focus more on getting in touch with yourself but absent from discerning how God is working in your life. Spiritual direction also helps you to know yourself, but only because when you have a deeper knowledge of your Creator, you will gain a deeper knowledge of yourself. Spiritual direction is primarily about forming, maintaining, and deepening a living encounter with God.

Would you like to have a person who listens to you and makes suggestions on spiritual matters? If so, how would you go about finding a spiritual director? There is no getting around the fact that finding a spiritual director can be difficult.

The best option is to first reach out to your parish priest and tell him you are considering spiritual direction. Ask, "Would you be able to be my spiritual director or can you recommend someone who could?" The second part of the question is important because the priest may be busy, and by asking for a recommendation, he will feel less pressure in telling you that he does not have enough time. (Also, while all priests are trained in spiritual direction, some do not feel called to this ministry.)

Another way to find a spiritual director is to be active in some way at a monastery or convent, perhaps by going on a retreat or participating in liturgies there. Consider asking someone you meet there if they could be your spiritual director (or recommend someone), most typically a monk or a nun.

Laypeople can also make very capable spiritual directors. You may have a connection with someone you know who prays, regularly attends the sacraments, and is well versed in spiritual reading. This might be a person you could ask. Your diocese likely has a formation program for spiritual directors too. If so, call the office and see if they have someone they could recommend.

I would prefer as few surprises at my particular judgment as possible. I want to know God in the deepest way in this life before I spend eternity contemplating his loving mystery. Having a spiritual director is one way to deepen my understanding of these things. And so, having a spiritual director is part of my plan for the future. I a m keeping my eyes and ears open now for a person who might fill that role for me, perhaps someone I can meet with once a month, either in person or online.

Although Jesus is the one who guides us to heaven, over the course of our lives we encounter many detours and roadblocks that we need help navigating. And yet we all wind up in one place: intertwined in the love of the Father, Son, and Holy Spirit and with Mary, the saints, and all our relatives and friends.

ACT IN THE PRESENT

Whereas spiritual direction is not intended to be a place to unburden ourselves of sin, this is precisely the purpose of the Sacrament of Reconciliation. Going to Confession should be a regular part of our faith lives.

When should we receive this sacrament? The Church requires us to go to Confession at least once a year (at Easter time; see *CCC* 1389), but you should also go any time you commit a mortal sin. These are sins that involve grave matters, full knowledge of the evil that took place, and full consent of will. Even if you committed the sin years ago, it's not too late to confess it. Now would be the perfect time to do so. The sacrament is also to remove venial or lesser sins that weaken and wound our relationship with God but do not destroy the grace in our soul.

There was a bit too much of one kind of rigidity on the sacrament prior to the Second Vatican Council. You may have heard of long lines of penitents lining up for Confession on Saturdays—every Saturday—and the same people in line. Catholics of that time were scrupulous in going to Confession because they believed any sin on their souls would keep them from receiving Communion on Sundays. My dad was like that. He worked on Saturdays and couldn't be one of the penitents who went to once-a-week Confession. So he did what he believed to be right; he remained in the pew and rarely received Holy Communion. The error my dad and others had during this period was thinking they could not receive Communion if they had committed *any* sin. The actual directive that remains the same today is that a person who has not confessed a *mortal* sin should not receive Communion. On the other hand, there is a different kind of moral error about Holy Communion today. There are many Catholics who receive Communion unworthily without having received absolution for a mortal sin in the Sacrament of Reconciliation.

There is nothing wrong with going to Confession frequently, including every Saturday. But if this habit seems unattainable for you now, consider two other markers to help you to remember and make time for Confession.

1. *Choose a set time each month.* You could go once a month, say, on the first Saturday of the month. In fact, Mary, in her apparition at Fatima, asked for Catholics to go to Confession on the first Saturdays for five consecutive months in reparation for sins against her Immaculate Heart. (Other

requirements of the first Saturday devotion are receiving Holy Communion, saying five decades of the Rosary, and keeping Mary company for fifteen minutes as you meditate on the other fifteen Mysteries of the Rosary.)

2. *Go four times each year if the once-a-month option for Confession is still too difficult for you to commit to right now.* There are four natural times to consider: once each during the penitential seasons of Lent and Advent, and then two other times, the beginning of summer (or end of the school year for you who have never given up a school schedule to guide your life) and the end of summer (or the start of the school year).

Some people who have been away from Confession for a number of years worry about the format and what they have to say. What you are responsible for is naming your sins (after recalling them through a thorough examination of conscience beforehand) and telling the priest you are sorry for them. Include some specifics, such as when it occurred and also whether it is something that is recurring.

For example, my recurrent sin has been gossiping. Weak, I know! I've been better at not sharing gossip myself, but I still have a problem with not walking away when gossip is being shared by another. By letting the priest know about the ongoing nature of this sin, he is better able to respond with a suggestion for helping me completely put an end to this occasion of sin.

The priest will also ask you to make an Act of Contrition. Personally, despite my public school upbringing, I still remember the Act of Contrition I learned in second grade CCD, complete with *thees* and *thous*. But if you don't remember, no worries. The priest will likely have a prayer card in the confessional with an Act of Contrition on it, or you can pray a prayer of sorrow for your sins in your own words. He will then give you some penance for your sins and you can be on your way.

God did not create us with sin in mind. Our Baptisms cleansed us from original sin. When we confess the sins we commit after Baptism, we draw ourselves again to the original holiness God intends for us and gain a better perspective on who we really are.

PRAY

> Examine yourself to see whether you are living
>   in faith.
> Test yourself.
> Realize that Jesus Christ is in you (unless you
>   fail the test).
> Pray to God that you do no evil.
> Do not take for granted that you have passed
>   the test.
> Seek forgiveness for your failings.
> Rejoice in your weakness, for it is then you seek
>   the Lord.
> Pray for your improvement.
> Test yourself.
>   —based on 2 Corinthians 13:5–9

REFLECT

- Who is someone you recognize for their holiness? Picture the occasion when his or her example of holiness was clearest to you.

- Describe your own process for seeking a spiritual director. Who might be your ideal spiritual director? What would you need from this person to help you learn more about God and yourself?

- Write down three reasons you should make going to Confession a scheduled part of your life.

2

PRAY REGULARLY

Prayer is a gift of God's grace—and is also a spiritual discipline we must cultivate through intentional, systematic effort. The moment we experience new life in Christ is also the moment when we begin a spiritual battle. By praying regularly, we aren't only fighting against our own laziness and poor resolve; Satan himself wants to keep us from our union with God in prayer.

As we grow older, the need for prayer does not diminish. We've already fought many battles and temptations in our lives and have faced Satan in other arenas. Now that we have more time, through regular prayer we can turn our attention to confront the evils we are currently facing and, with God's help, defeat them now and up until the moment of death.

REMEMBER THE PAST

Throughout my life, my conversations with God have experienced ebbs and flows. One of the high points of my prayer life occurred in the months when I first started dating my wife, Lisa. I consciously made time in prayer before the Blessed Sacrament to ask Jesus to bless this budding relationship and to keep it going. I knew I wanted to marry Lisa long before I had the courage to let her know of this desire. God seemed so close to me in prayer during those days, and he graciously answered this prayer in the affirmative.

However, there were plenty of other times, before and after this occasion, when I skipped regular prayer. In fact, how I have approached God in prayer over the years has some strong similarities with the dynamics I experience as a father with my own children.

I'll explain it this way: My firstborn, Alexandra Marie, was a "Daddy's girl" by my design. I took Alex everywhere. I pushed her in her stroller to the library. I found new parks where she could try out her favorite rings and jungle gyms. When I was a youth minister at St. Monica's, I took her to work with me, and the teenagers doted over her. St. Monica's was attended by several Hollywood celebrities, and when Lucie Arnaz requested a memorial Mass for her mom, Lucille Ball, Alex and I had a seat in the third-row pew. Then we walked home and watched an episode of *I Love Lucy*, one of our favorite shows.

When I did go to work without Alex, I would look back at the house from the driveway and see her face pressed against the front window. Even if I got home late, Alex would never be in a deep sleep and would always give me a sigh and a smile as I tucked her blankets back in. If I was home when she went to bed, she would say, "Daddy, rustle the newspaper so that I know you are there." We had a tight bond. And then, overnight, it seemed, we didn't. Somewhere in middle school, the girl who could repeat back any detailed story I had shared with her about the Beatles, her grandmother, how I met her mom, Jesus, and the saints, now only answered me with three or four words.

"Alex, how was school today?"

"FINE." (Make that one word.)

Everyone said that things would improve, that all kids go through this phase with their parents. I certainly had, too. But I missed the deep connection I used to have with Alexandra Marie. So I watched from more of a distance as she interacted with her friends, played sports, and just plain grew up.

When she went off to college, I actually was looking forward to more depth to our conversations than we had experienced while Alex was in high school. This was also around the time that I owned my first cell phone. I figured that with these new two-way magical contraptions it would be easy for me to stay connected with my daughter. But just like with a landline, most of the calls to Alex took three or four tries to get picked up. When she did answer, the conversations remained plain, basic, and short. Still, I remember that when I did talk to Alex, I was just glad to hear her voice and to be able to recognize through it that she was happy and doing well.

I can't pinpoint the exact occasion when things changed again. I do remember that after Alex had moved to New York, she met me one night at Penn Station where I was coming in to see her after spending a day working in Philadelphia. We went out to a restaurant she had picked out. The food was unmemorable. But Alex was different. We talked about lots of things: the students in her eighth-grade math class, her friends in Hoboken who also had a cottage on the Jersey Shore, how she would help to take care of her youngest brother if anything happened to me and her mom, and why she wasn't going to Mass on Sundays but that she still prayed and might go again to Mass someday. Not all of the conversation was what I wanted to hear, but at least there was lots of it.

In those times and in the years since, whenever I would fret or celebrate the up and down nature of communication between my oldest child and me, I also think about how similar it is with my prayer conversations with God. (Cast me as "Alex" and God as "Father" with a capital *F*.)

Through the first years of life, I prayed to God with a child's love and devotion. When did things change? I'm not exactly sure, but I do note the difference between how excited I was as a seven-year-old to receive first Holy Communion compared to how put off I was about having to miss a little league game on my Confirmation day when I was twelve. At that point I was ignoring God; we had only a perfunctory relationship for the next several years. I wonder what he thought of me when I was distant from him? He was probably like a dad watching his daughter grow up from the outskirts while patiently waiting for her to return to communion with him.

As with any parent with a child, God wants to be in constant dialogue with us in prayer, but he accepts what we will give him until we can give him more. There is an example of this shared in John's gospel when the risen Jesus met with seven disciples along the shore of the Sea of Tiberias. After eating breakfast, Jesus said to Peter, "Simon, son of John, do you love me more than these?" (Jn 21:15). The word for love used in the Greek translation of John's gospel is *agape*, the most intimate form of love. Agape is also a sacrificial form of love. Peter responds, "Yes, Lord, you know that I love you." (Jn 21:16). Except for Peter's response, the Greek translation of scripture uses *phile*, a word meaning love for a friend. Jesus asks the question a second time, again using the word *agape*. Peter again responds with *phile*.

Jesus asks the question one more time, "Simon, son of John, do you *phile*?" Jesus has restated the question in Peter's terms. Jesus has met Peter directly. If, for the present moment, Peter could not offer Jesus the kind of love Jesus was seeking, Jesus would accept what Peter could give. I know as parents we sometimes do the same with our children. I wish my daughter would meet me for Mass on Sunday morning. But even when she won't on this day doesn't mean I won't agree to have dinner with her on Sunday evening.

Our own prayer life has similar ebbs and flows. Sometimes we are unable to give ourselves completely to God in prayer. But we are not to give up.

PLAN FOR THE FUTURE

I recently saw a funny pie chart on social media. About 99.9 percent of the circle was shaded in blue. The code explained that the blue signified "the time spent choosing a movie to stream." The other small sliver of red was labeled "the time actually spent watching the movie." Seems about right. There have been plenty of days when that small sliver represents the time I've devoted to prayer, and the large section of blue represents things like watching Netflix or thinking about the drop in my 401(k).

Recently, I've been trying to add *minutes* and *meaning* to my prayer time. It's a natural instinct for a Christian to want to pray more. There are some days, in fact, when I want to fill in all or just about all of that pie chart with prayer, in agreement with St. John Vianney, the famous Cur de Ars, who once said,

> The more we pray, the more we wish to pray. Like a fish that at first swims on the surface of the water, and afterwards plunges down, and is always going deeper; the soul plunges, dives, and loses itself in the sweetness of conversing with God.[1]

In recent years, I've found that prayer focuses my thoughts, motivations, and actions on Jesus. The more I pray, the less I think or care about political debates. The more I pray, the less I care that the guy two doors down is violating the neighborhood covenant by keeping his trash cans in front of his garage door instead of on the side of his house. Prayer seems to have replaced the news media for me in every way. In prayer I feel more in touch with the Good News than the cable news.

The Church has a dedicated formula for round-the-clock prayer. It's the Church's official public prayer, the Divine Office or Liturgy of the Hours. Its plan of ritual for prayer is to fill the entire day and night and has been a practice ever since Old Testament times. Jews prayed regularly from the Psalter, a liturgical book made up primarily of the Psalms. This type of prayer was done both in public, in the synagogue, and privately in a special sacred place designated in the home. Jesus himself prayed in this way.

In the early days of the Church, Christians prayed round the clock, sometimes in hiding in the catacombs since Christianity was illegal and punishable by death. The third hour after dawn

(9 a.m.), the sixth hour (noon), and the ninth hour (3 p.m.) were designated as times for private prayer.

By the time Christianity was legalized in the fourth century, monastic communities began to adopt the practice of reciting prayers throughout the day and into the night. In the eighth century, the Church brought uniformity to the Divine Office with prayers, readings, and songs compiled from several sources, including the Psalter, the Book of Prophets, the Book of the Law, the Antiphonary (book of chants), the Martyrology (acts of martyrs), and the Sanctoral (calendar of saints). Eventually, these materials were abbreviated into one book, a *breviary*, that was officially commissioned by the Council of Trent in the sixteenth century. The breviary has been modified at other times since—including by St. Pius X in the early twentieth century and after the Second Vatican Council—with new translations and the combination or removal of some feast days of saints.

The Divine Office most commonly consists of an hour of scripture readings, Morning Prayer, midday prayer, Evening Prayer, and a short night prayer. A breviary or an online accompaniment to the Divine Office helps to make praying the Divine Office less confusing.

I've started praying the Office gradually, beginning with Morning Prayer and Evening Prayer. I pray the Morning Prayer with my headphones on while I shave, brush my teeth, and get dressed. I pray the Evening Prayer after eating dinner. I take myself to a quiet room once populated by one of my kids and pray the Evening Prayer at a less rushed pace through listening and reading. About half of the nights during the week I also pray a night prayer in bed, especially when I am having trouble going to sleep. The Morning Prayer and Evening Prayer each take about thirty minutes. The shorter night prayer is about ten minutes. I do fall asleep sometimes before completing it.

I don't just want to pray more in the future, I want to pray better. I don't want to only "pray words"; I want to reflect on what I am praying. St. Teresa of Ávila said, "A prayer in which a person is not aware of Whom he is speaking to, what he is asking, who it is who is asking and of Whom, I don't call prayer—however much the lips may move."[2]

But I really do want to pray more too; I want to fill up that pie chart because I have a funny feeling that the entry-level position in heaven will be to pray. Do you think you have relatives in heaven who are praying for you? Our joint membership in the Communion of Saints would seem to suggest this common task. St. Thérèse of Lisieux wrote in her journal, "Upon my death I will let fall a shower of roses; I wish to spend my heaven in doing good upon the earth."[3] The good we can do then, as now, is through prayer.

ACT IN THE PRESENT

The more we pray, the more it increases our understanding of God's agape love, and the better we can give that same kind of love back to him and to others. True, like any loving parent, God will wait for us to be open to the depth and breadth of his love. But it is our time *now* to put aside talking as a child, thinking as a child, and reasoning as a child and instead speak to God face-to-face, often, and with clarity.

Could prayer be the most important activity that takes place in the world? Think of the nuns and priests who live in mostly silence and yet who share in a constant twenty-four hours of prayer through the night and day. In a fictional short story, "In the Convent Chapel," early twentieth-century author Msgr. Robert Hugh Benson describes the experience of a priest as he watches a contemplative nun at prayer and comes to understand that

> in my stupid arrogance I had thought that my life
> was more active in God's world then hers. . . . There
> lay my little foolish narrow life behind me, made up
> of spiritless prayers and efforts and feeble dealings
> with souls; and how complacent I had been with it all,
> how self-centered, how out of the real tide of spiritual

> movement! And meanwhile, for years probably, this
> nun had toiled behind these walls in the silence of
> grace, with the hum of the world coming faintly to
> her ears, and the cries of the peoples and nations,
> and of persons whom the world accounts import-
> ant, sounding like the voices of children at play in
> the muddy street outside; and indeed that is all they
> are, compared to her—children making mud-pies or
> playing shop outside the financier's office.[4]

Today, I make time for prayer and do it more thoughtfully.
Before being able to dedicate myself to the complete application
of the Divine Office, I continue to use a hybrid version. With the
Morning Prayer, I also pray a decade of the Rosary. At lunch-
time, usually in my car, I keep the radio off until I complete the
Angelus.

Sometime after 3 p.m., I pray the Chaplet of Divine Mercy.
This is the prayer that Jesus revealed to St. Faustina Kowalska,
a Polish nun, just after World War II. St. John Paul II himself
prayed the chaplet, which is a recitation of prayers on rosary
beads, to help us, in the words of St. Faustina, to pray to Jesus to

> be mindful of Your own bitter Passion and do not
> permit the loss of souls redeemed at so dear a price of
> Your most precious Blood. O Jesus, when I consider
> the great price of Your Blood, I rejoice at its immen-
> sity, for one drop alone would have been enough for
> the salvation of all sinners.[5]

Whether we do fourteen or fourteen hundred things before
we die to make ourselves better Catholics, we will ultimately
rely on God's mercy to save us. His mercy is incomprehensible
and inexhaustible. The Chaplet of Divine Mercy, said even once,
will guarantee that we sinners will receive grace from the Lord's
infinite mercy. If possible, pray the chaplet between 3 p.m. and
4 p.m., the hour that Jesus hung on the Cross.

For now, I've constructed my night prayer to align with the Divine Office, with the option of reserving some nights for different types of spiritual reading, including the lives of the saints, seasonal prayer programs, and of course praying directly from the Bible. It all sounds good on paper. Now to put it into action.

PRAY

> Be at peace among yourselves.
> Admonish the idle.
> Cheer the fainthearted.
> Support the weak.
> Be patient with all.
> Rejoice always.
> Pray without ceasing.
> In all circumstances, give thanks,
> for this is the will of God for you in Christ Jesus.
> —based on 1 Thessalonians 5:13–18

REFLECT

- In what part of your day could you carve out thirty minutes of dedicated prayer time? Imagine an ideal setting for your prayer. What does it look like? What type of prayer will you choose for those thirty minutes?

- List five other times and places during the day when you can make time for God, for example, in the car on the way to work, at lunch under a tree, or after dinner in a comfortable chair.

- What is a new prayer form you would like to practice on a regular basis? When would it best fit in your schedule? Take time to pencil it in right now for the coming week.

3

ATTEND DAILY MASS

When we are at Mass, it is as if we are truly present at the actual events of the Last Supper, Good Friday, and the Resurrection of Jesus. Pope Francis said, "The Mass is the memorial of Jesus' Passover of his 'exodus,' which he carried out for us, so as to lead us out of slavery and introduce us to he promised land of eternal life. It is not merely a remembrance, no. It is more: it is making present what happened twenty centuries ago."[1]

As we draw close to these mysteries, we transcend time in a way that is similar to what we will experience when we leave this earth: we will be outside of the confines of time. Thankfully, we can experience this as much as possible by attending daily Mass and encountering the Real Presence of Jesus. If you want to get ready for eternal life, cultivating the habit of daily Mass is a great way to do it.

REMEMBER THE PAST

My draw toward daily Mass and the Mass in general happened in fifth grade, when I trained to be an altar boy (known today as "altar server"). Each time I served at Mass, I heard scripture and the lessons of the priest shared in the homily, and I learned something more about Jesus and the faith. My experiences serving at Mass also advanced my identity as a Catholic. I felt more a part of the whole thing and a true participant in the Church.

On one hand, the attraction to be an altar boy was pragmatic. There were some basic rewards that were in play for a ten-year-old. We had to serve a certain number of daily Masses to qualify for an altar boy trip to the Pickwood Recreation Center, held on a school day later in the year. My altar boy partner, Joe Perfetto, and I were public school kids, so we had few chances to be called on for extra daily Masses, unlike our counterparts at St. Luke's School. Joe and I needed to have a corner on the summer 8 a.m. Masses, and that we did.

One week in July, there were funerals on Monday and Tuesday. There wasn't much difference between a funeral Mass and a regular Mass except we had to fill the aspergillum (we called it a "shaker" in 1968) with water so the priest could bless the casket at the conclusion of Mass. One time, Joe—he still says it was me—didn't screw the top of the shaker on tight enough and it flew off when Fr. Holland was on his third of three shakes. He was embarrassed when it happened, and not pleased with us when we got back to the sacristy.

Fr. Holland was also the priest for the Monday and Tuesday funerals. On both days, as Joe and I knelt in the sacristy for his blessing after Mass, Father flipped us each a Kennedy half-dollar. Funerals did not pay as much as weddings, of course, but fifty cents was definitely a nice benefit: it could buy ten packs of baseball cards, five sodas, and much more. Lo and behold, on Wednesday there was a third funeral! Telepathy was strong between Joe and me during Mass, planning our stop at the drug store candy counter using our latest payment. However, Fr. Holland switched it up. Wednesday brought only his blessing, no silver coin.

"Father obviously just forgot to give us our fifty cents," Joe said to me after Mass. "Go knock on the rectory door and remind him." It was a textbook case of peer pressure—and I blew it. I went up and knocked on the door . . . and Joe sped off on his Sting-Ray and was halfway up Cloverly Avenue by the time Fr.

Holland got done admonishing me for asking for money, his breakfast napkin still dangling from his clericals.

In addition to these tangible rewards were other more sanctifying lessons I learned from being an altar boy at daily Mass. The Mass of Paul VI, which replaced the Tridentine Mass, removed the requirements for altar boys to recite in Latin the prayers at the foot of the altar, so we had fewer "jobs" to learn and do during Mass. But one big job remained—the ringing of the bells at the time of the consecration—and Joe and I both wanted to do it.

Carefully, we passed the golden chime along the kneeler between the lifting up of the host and the lifting up of the chalice so that we each got a turn. But who would get to ring the bells the third time? Before reciting the words of Jesus from the Last Supper, the priest stretched his hands over the bread and wine and one of us would need to ring the bells then too. We kept careful records of whose Mass it was to get to ring the bells this extra time.

As I got older and began to pay attention and better understand the Mass, I never forgot the focus we had as altar boys on the priest's extension of his hands. What we didn't quite care to grasp then was that this was actually the climactic moment of the Mass, when the priest calls on the Holy Spirit—the Third Person of the Blessed Trinity—to undertake the transubstantiation of the regular, plain white hosts made of bread and regular table wine into the Body and Blood of Jesus. It is a belief that the invocation of the Holy Spirit and recitation of Jesus's words of consecration bring about Jesus's Real Presence that makes us unique as Catholics.

PLAN FOR THE FUTURE

I want to be counted as a "daily Mass-goer." As a kid, my mom used such a term with great respect. Our neighbor up the street, Al Goetz from Pittsburgh, went to morning Mass every day, and he was a kind man who was rarely apart from his son Danny who had Down syndrome. Vince Lombardi, the great Green Bay Packers coach, went to daily Mass both in season and offseason. When the city named a street after him near the church, Lombardi made all thirty-seven officials who attended the ceremony go to Mass with him first.

I never fear not having a "place to go" after I retire from full-time work because I will go to daily Mass. I will have a reason to get out of bed, get dressed, and start the car. It will be to go to Mass. Once there, I'll find other regular Mass-goers. In fact, it seems that in the last few years, there are more people at daily Mass than in recent times, a purely anecdotal comment. I'm the kind of person who can have my need for community fulfilled at Mass just by seeing the same people, nodding to them at the sign of peace, and commenting to them on the weather or Notre Dame football news on the way to the parking lot. But some people develop a more intentional community among daily Mass-goers. You may have seen such a group sharing doughnuts at a local bakery or a full breakfast at a diner near your parish church on a weekday morning.

At daily Mass, I'll be able to follow a longer cycle of connected readings, and after three years of going to daily Mass, I will have heard a good portion of the Bible. As with Sundays, I like to hear scripture readings that have been chosen by the Church and that are the same readings being shared worldwide. God speaks his Word in scripture regardless, but it seems that his providence can often be detected in a reading that is particularly chosen by the Church for that exact day. Also, at daily Mass the homilies seem to be more to the point than on Sundays. I once told my priest friend that I liked his daily homilies better than his Sunday homilies for that reason: they homed right in on what was important instead of the embellishments the parishioners expect with the Sunday homilies (e.g., icebreakers, parish announcements, topical sermons).

The main reason I want to go to daily Mass is that Jesus is always there, and at the time of Holy Communion, he is as close to me as possible. Jesus makes this very clear when he speaks of himself as the Bread of Life:

> I am the living bread that came down from heaven; whoever eats this bread will live forever; and the bread that I will give is my flesh for the life of the world. . . . Amen, amen, I say to you, unless you eat the flesh of the Son of Man and drink his blood, you do not have life within you. Whoever eats my flesh and drinks my blood has eternal life, and I will raise him on the last day. For my flesh is true food, and my blood is true drink. Whoever eats my flesh and drinks my blood remains in me and I in him. (Jn 6:51, 53–56)

Holy Communion *should* be received as much as possible. It isn't a magic potion, but it is the source of eternal life. St. Pius X was instrumental in reframing the understanding of reception of Holy Communion so that more Catholics would come to the altar and receive Jesus. The pope permitted children to receive the Eucharist at the age of reason (around the age of seven) rather than make their First Communion around the age of twelve. He emphasized that only the commission of mortal sin without reception of absolution in the Sacrament of Reconciliation should keep a Catholic from receiving Holy Communion. He summed up his teachings in one of my favorite hopeful quotations:

> Holy Communion is the shortest and safest way to heaven. There are others: innocence, but that is for children; penance, but we are afraid of it; generous endurance of the trials of life, but when they come we weep and ask to be spared. The surest, easiest, shortest way is the Eucharist.[2]

I don't mind taking a shortcut when I can, and so be it if it is Mass that is the shortcut. I am again reminded of how Jesus has come to make our yoke easy and our burden light.

ACT IN THE PRESENT

When our kids were starting to explore where to go to college, we established a rule of sorts: you can go to any in-state public college, or you can go to any Catholic college in America except for Boston College. (Boston College cost Notre Dame a national football championship in 1993. Not forgiven.) Ellen, like her brother Tony, chose Marquette, a Jesuit university in Milwaukee. Unlike her brother, who went to a Catholic high school, Ellen graduated from a public high school. In the beginning, I was excited that Ellen would take a course in Catholicism in her first semester at Marquette. But then there was a curriculum change and *oops!* suddenly students could choose any religion course among many selections. Ellen chose a class on Eastern religions; she never had a single class on Catholicism or Christianity in four years at Marquette.

Even so, we never regretted encouraging our kids to go to Catholic colleges. Why? These schools have chapels on campus with the red sanctuary lamp burning to indicate Jesus is there, present in the Blessed Sacrament. In fact, upon helping Ellen move out from her dorm after her first year, I happened to open a door in the lobby where I discovered the smallest chapel I had ever seen. All it had was one kneeler, a tabernacle, and the lit sanctuary lamp. I made Ellen stop and poke her head inside. "Did you know this was here?" She didn't. "Just to let you know, this little room is why I pay my share of the tuition! Make yourself at home here next semester!"

When we don't have time to go to Mass on a particular day, why not make time for Eucharistic Adoration? This long-held practice in the Church is also known as a Holy Hour, where we sit or kneel before Jesus in the Blessed Sacrament and ask him to look thoughtfully and lovingly at us while we look at him in the same way. This practice is an extension of Mass.

The first occasion of Eucharistic Adoration is actually *at* Mass when the priest holds up the consecrated host before Communion and says, "Behold, the Lamb of God, behold him who takes away the sins of the world." Yet this time to see the uplifted host is much too brief. More time is needed to be with the Lord after Mass has ended. Since at least the fourth century, perpetual adoration has been a practice in the Church. Entire religious communities are devoted to making sure that someone is always present before the Eucharist in devotion. Perhaps your parish has sponsored something similar—a forty-hour devotion that is often held in combination with parish mission or retreat.

There are things you can *do* during Eucharistic Adoration besides just sitting there in silence. You can read from the Bible or other spiritual readings. You can pray devotional prayers like the Rosary. Personally, I prefer to remain quiet. I focus on the tabernacle or, if exposed, the Blessed Sacrament in the monstrance. Sometimes I repeat a mantra to myself. Lately, the gift of the Lord's mercy has been on my mind, so I say something to myself like, "Jesus, have mercy on me" or, in Latin, "Kyrie, eleison." I also have been very fortunate since the time I left home for college in 1975 to always have the Blessed Sacrament nearby to where I worked or lived: across the street from my office today at Moreau Seminary, Notre Dame; in the beautiful St. Monica's Church in Santa Monica where I worked for fourteen years after college; and, yes, in my own chapel dorm in Whelan Hall at Loyola Marymount University. My other mantra is "Thanks be to God" for this great gift of Jesus's Real Presence.

PRAY

> I am the bread of life.
> Come to me.
> You will not hunger.
> You will not thirst.
> Everyone who sees me and believes in me will
>   have eternal life.
> You will rise on the last day.

You are the bread of life.
Amen.

—based on John 6:34–40

REFLECT

- How might you fit daily Mass into your schedule? Where will you attend? What time will you choose?

- Research and write down five quotations by saints about the Real Presence of Christ in the Eucharist. Pray with them at Eucharistic Adoration.

- Rank the benefits that you think you would gain by attending daily Mass. Why did you rank your top reason as you did?

4
STUDY SCRIPTURE

Reading the Bible and understanding the meaning of scripture is one of the most important ways we can hear the voice of God. St. Jerome famously wrote, "Ignorance of the Scriptures is ignorance of Christ" (as quoted in *CCC* 24). Likewise, St. Augustine of Hippo noted "that one and the same Word of God extends throughout Scripture" and that one Word is Christ.[1]

As Catholics, we have access to many resources—many of which were not available to previous generations—to guide us in our ongoing exercise of prayerful dialogue and study. These books and other resources make accessible the treasury of our faith; each succeeding generation has something to teach us about sacred scripture. Take a moment to ask for the Holy Spirit's guidance, the One who inspired the biblical writers, to gently lead you to do regular reading and to direct you to a program of study of sacred scripture, whether it be in a formal course, in a parish group, or on your own.

REMEMBER THE PAST

My parents didn't have a Bible in our house. My uncle, who had a desk full of pamphlets written by Archbishop Fulton J. Sheen and information about the apparitions of Mary to the children at Fatima, didn't have a Bible either. After first-grade CCD, where my teacher accompanied Bible stories with characters she moved around on a piece of burlap, I entered a personal void of what I knew and what I thought I was allowed to know about the Bible. This was ironic, too, because the changes wrought by the Second Vatican Council were in full force, including a revision of the liturgy that intended to include even more scripture readings over a three-year cycle.

Slowly and carefully through the twentieth century, the Church opened herself to a more thorough study of scripture by theologians and scholars while also beginning to encourage all Catholics to read, study, and especially pray with the Bible. The council document *Dei Verbum* said that "easy access to Sacred Scripture should be provided for all the Christian faithful" (22). New Catholic translations of the Bible blossomed after the council, most with outstanding study notes to help readers learn the context of particular biblical books and passages. But the process was slow, and remains slow, for some Catholics to even have a Bible in their possession, much less reading, studying, and praying with it.

In public school back in those days, we sang Christmas carols with lyrics inspired by scripture passages right along with the Protestant kids. And in 1965, when I was in Mrs. Blakeley's third-grade class, a new Christmas program debuted on prime-time television. It was *A Charlie Brown Christmas*, written and produced by Charles M. Schultz, a nominal Lutheran. The show itself was a little too esoteric at the time for my third-grade self (Lucy as a psychologist and all), but it ended with a climactic scene in which the character Linus tells of the birth of Christ in a reading from the King James edition of the Gospel of Luke. I can remember wondering what exactly he was quoting from. The Bible? Is this what the priest read from at Sunday Mass? I hadn't realized. It was also a bit confusing to hear a kid—and a cartoon character at that—reading these holy words. I thought only a priest could do that.

More biblical confusion emerged for me in junior high and high school. This was the early 1970s, and I did learn later that Bibles were only beginning to make an appearance in Catholic high school theology classes. Some Catholic schools purchased classroom sets of abridged Bibles or Bibles written in a colloquial style that often only included the New Testament.

In public school, we had social studies class, not theology. I had courses focusing on traditional American history in fifth grade, Central and South America in sixth grade, and something called "Ancient Mesopotamia" in seventh grade. It was seventh grade that threw me off. I couldn't figure out how this Mesopotamian society fit in context with what I knew on a peripheral level as "biblical times." Neither the textbook nor the teacher ever mentioned any of the biblical characters I had some knowledge of: Abraham, Moses, and King David. The year left me with a feeling that what I was learning in seventh-grade social studies was *fact*, what I was picking up in the first reading at Sunday Mass was *fiction*. This was a dangerous proposition for a young Catholic.

By the start of high school, I still hadn't held a Bible in my hands to read from it. Finally, in my junior year, we were given an assignment in a literature class to read from Genesis about Joseph, his brothers, his colorful coat, and at last, in my mind, some backstory on who the Hebrew people were and how they had ended up as slaves in Egypt. Remember, my family didn't have a Bible in our home. I can still picture the exact corner of the public library where I was sitting on a weeknight opening a reference Bible and reading God's Word for the first time for a public high school assignment. The story was fascinating; the writing, exceptional. It certainly left me wanting more chances to read from the Bible.

Hurrah (in this case) for Jesuit higher education! In my freshman year at Loyola Marymount University, I enrolled in two theology classes. One was an introduction to Catholicism. The other was called "Foundations of Christianity" with an expert and inspiring teacher named Fr. Herb Ryan, SJ, who required the purchase of the *New American Bible* as one of the course texts. In my mind, this meant that reading the Bible on my own was "Catholic approved," and soon I was off and running with personal Bible reading and study. I marked up this Bible with notes and underlined passages I wanted to ask Fr. Ryan about or to research later myself. From that point on, I continued to look for classes with a scripture focus, into graduate school and beyond, for personal enrichment through online noncredit courses. I also began a habit of keeping the Bible near my bed and reading it at night before going to sleep.

PLAN FOR THE FUTURE

There are three different types of Bible study I am looking forward to doing again. I say *again* because I've had a brief taste of each kind in the past.

I'd like to take another academic course in biblical scholarship. I took the first one in graduate school as part of a degree program and appreciated the seriousness of the format at the time, the high-level discussions, written term papers, exams, and, yes, grades. If I were to take a class like that now, I wouldn't feel the same pressure to pass the course, or to get a gold star on an exam or paper. I just like the formality of this type of class and the impression it communicated that biblical studies was a serious academic discipline.

One course I took was particularly eye-opening. It was taught by a Protestant professor from Claremont College named Dr. Robert Miller. There were only four other students in the class, all nuns from the same religious community. We sat around in separate desks arranged in a rectangle and went through the gospels each week over three hours. Most of the focus for the semester was on what I learned was likely the first gospel written, the Gospel of Mark.

The mastery of the author, Mark, in constructing the gospel remains unforgettable to me. The gospel had "good" characters and "bad" characters, literary devices I had never learned as an undergraduate English major, and a mystery focus revolving around Jesus's true identity, which was kept hidden from just about everyone except for us, the careful readers. The entire gospel was set as a journey as Jesus made his way to Jerusalem where he would fulfill his mission as King, but not in a way that anybody expected.

One of Mark's literary techniques was to highlight important passages by "framing" them in the middle of an introductory and concluding story with the same topic or theme. The best I can do to explain this is with a comparison one of my classmates, Sr. Ann Joseph, made between Mark's use of this framing literary technique and a similar one used in the early episodes of *Seinfeld*. You may remember the early *Seinfeld* shows begin with Jerry doing his comedy routine in a nightclub, followed by the main plot of the episode, and then ending with another nightclub clip. Mark used a similar approach in several different places in his gospel.

Take the incident recorded in Mark 11:12–14 where Jesus curses a fig tree. It seems Jesus went to the tree looking for something to eat, though it wasn't the season for figs to be ripe. Jesus says directly to the tree, "May no one ever eat of your fruit again!" Remember, it wasn't fig season so the astute reader may wonder why Jesus would be surprised and angry that there were no figs. If you look at what comes before and after this incident, there may be a clue to its meaning.

Before and after the incident with the fig tree are two stories of Jesus in the Temple. In both stories there are expectations and reverberations among his followers that these appearances in the Temple area were the time and occasion when Jesus would initiate his rule and take power. But that didn't happen on either trip to the Temple. Why? Biblical scholarship suggests looking to the story of the fig tree that appears between the two Temple stories. Sr. Ann Joseph solved the mystery for our class: Just as it wasn't time for figs, it wasn't yet the time for the events of Jesus's Passion, Death, and Resurrection that would coronate him as our king and bring about our salvation when he made those two trips to the Temple.

Mark's technique was to place the story of the fig tree in a place where its lesson could be uncovered with investigation and reflection. Just as we are more likely to remember the main episode, not the comedy routines in *Seinfeld*, Mark intends for us to remember the *lesson* of the fig tree, not what went on at the Temple. At least this was the explanation of Dr. Miller. The four nuns and I discussed and researched other framing stories in the Gospel of Mark. I enjoyed the speculation.

Another thing I liked about this academic course was that in learning about the method of scripture study classified as "historical criticism," we were able to determine the probability of what parts of the gospels' reports can be traced directly to Jesus without any additions of later oral storytellers, authors, or editors. Using historical criticism, the following three assumptions are made:

- *Linguistic analysis.* Since Jesus spoke Aramaic, gospel verses containing Aramaic words or passages can likely be traced directly to Jesus. Examples are *Abba* ("Father"), *Talitha koum* ("Little girl, get up"), and *Eloi, Eloi, lema sabachthani* ("My God, my God, why have you forsaken me?"). Does evidence that these words can be proven to come directly from the mouth of the Son of God bolster your faith? It does mine.

- *Criterion of dissimilarity.* This argument holds that anything Jesus said that was unique and apart from the Jewish and early Christian traditions and culture of that time is probably unique to him. His parables meet this criterion. There are no examples of them in any other sources of the time.

- *Convergence of sources.* The gospels of Mathew and Luke were written independently of each other, yet they both state that Jesus was born during the reign of Herod the Great and in the town of Bethlehem. They include other compatible details as well. This is evidence of the accuracy of this information.

You were once a student, and maybe you remember what it was like to do thorough research and study. Or maybe you have more recent careful reading experience in your profession or trade. These types of experiences qualify you to enroll in a challenging scripture study course. Don't shy away from it because you're concerned you will feel out of place. I'll bet that at least half of the people enrolled in these types of courses will be heading for the finish line of life just as we are. You can participate in a scripture course either online or in person, preferably through a Catholic college, institute, or diocesan adult education program. Such a course will give you confidence in your understanding of scripture and help you to drill even deeper to the core of knowing Jesus than you may have thought possible.

ACT IN THE PRESENT

Do you find the idea of an academic scripture class intimidating (or boring)? Let me suggest two other types of scripture study that have a bit more flexibility as a place to begin sooner rather than later.

First, read the Bible on your own. I just mentioned one recent TV sitcom, so let me bring up another. Patricia Heaton, who played Debra on *Everybody Loves Raymond* (and also Frankie on *The Middle*), recently spent 365 straight days reading the Bible from cover to cover. Part of her reading involved praying and meditating with passages, but a lot of it was pure study. Patricia said that she took notes on her daily reading and used the footnoted references to gain context for the passages. In the back of her Bible, she made a list of all of the various titles used for God, such as "Healer," "Provider," and "Good Shepherd."

"Some days were revelatory," she said. "I saw things that I had never seen before. And some days were kind of a slog . . . especially in parts of the Old Testament."[2] After she finished, Patricia said she would formulate a new plan for reading the Bible that didn't go from beginning to end but instead focused on themes or particular biblical books.

If you choose to do an individual study of the Bible, I don't recommend the cover-to-cover method. Choosing one particular book to study, for example, is usually a great first approach. One of the gospels is a good bet. Gather some resources to accompany the study. There are several excellent biblical commentaries you can use. Make sure to choose Catholic commentaries as the Catholic approach to understanding the Bible differs from most Protestant approaches.

What time of day will you do your reading? Try to keep to the schedule. Choose smaller sections to study over larger ones. This will give you more time to digest what you have read and make its application to your life. Finally, keep a journal, either in a separate source or in the page margins of your bible. If the latter, underline passages that have special meaning to you or that you want to research at a later time. If the former, write meaningful passages in your journal along with a reflective note on why you found the passage important.

Second, consider joining a group study. Your parish likely sponsors a scripture group for study and prayer. These groups sometimes come together in liturgical seasons. Maybe your parish has a Lenten group that meets on Fridays to share a simple meal and then break open one of the penitential readings of the season. Other times, a weekend parish retreat or mission will naturally lead to forming small prayer and study groups after the conclusion of the main event.

Here's an important suggestion: next time you see an announcement in the parish program promoting a scripture lecture, prayer service, retreat, discussion, or whatever else might come after the word "scripture," show some new confidence and take the parish up on its offer. Be bold and try out a new experience.

One last pro tip: Years ago when I first started teaching at the parish school, one of my coworkers told me that she and her friends had regular revolving Sunday-night dinners and that I was invited. To me, it sounded like a party, though I do believe she mentioned that there would be prayer and discussion with the dinner. Later in the week, she gave me a handwritten invitation to that week's dinner with the initials BYOB at the bottom. So, not being a person who drinks hard liquor, I brought a six-pack of the latest craft beer. Once I arrived at the private home of a couple I had never met and before my teacher friend who invited me arrived, I noticed the troubled faces when I unpacked my brown sack with the beer. I quickly realized that the second "B" referred to my Bible, not my bottles of beer. You've been warned!

PRAY

> Blessed are you, O Lord,
>   teach me your ways.
> With my lips I recite
>   all that you have taught me.
> I find joy in the way of your words
>   more than in all riches.
> I will ponder your words
>   and consider your ways.
> In your words I take delight:
> I will never forget your word.
>   —based on Psalm 119:9–16

REFLECT

- What are your first memories of reading and praying with the Bible?

- How do you understand the differences between how Catholics and Protestants interpret and understand the Bible?

- Which type of scripture study sounds like something you might want to do in the future: an academic course, group study, or individual study? Why? How would you pursue the option you prefer?

5

MAKE A PILGRIMAGE

For Catholics, a pilgrimage is different from a road trip or a visit to a history or art museum. It is both a physical and a spiritual journey. Catholics in every age have made visits to holy sites like the Holy Land, Rome, Lourdes, and Fatima. You've likely read Chaucer's *Canterbury Tales*. The interesting characters you encountered were on a pilgrimage to visit a shrine to St. Thomas Becket. They, as with us who make a pilgrimage today, expect to be spiritually transformed. We expect to meet God in places where he once was clearly revealed.

Is the desire to be a pilgrim part of our own God-given nature? Abraham, our father in faith, went on one, taking his family to an unknown land at God's request. God himself made the ultimate pilgrimage, leaving his throne in heaven for a straw manger in Bethlehem. Maybe planning and undertaking a pilgrimage is indeed ingrained in us.

REMEMBER THE PAST

Yes, a pilgrimage is different from a road trip. I made plenty of road trips during the pandemic, especially during the weeks of the severest lockdowns. Freedoms curtailed, I felt trapped. Restaurants, stadiums, churches (sadly), and even some parks were closed. It was a miserable time. I wondered, where could I go? Eventually, I started taking drives on Saturdays. I checked a map and looked for destinations fifty to a hundred miles away from home. Maybe there would be a nature reserve or a state park open on the other end where I could get out and stretch my legs. In the car I went, classic rock on the radio up on full blast, windows down. I needed to go *somewhere*. But these drives were not pilgrimages.

I experienced something closer to pilgrimage—a road trip with a central spiritual component—when I was eighteen years old, just after my freshman year of college. It was America's bicentennial, 1976, and the Summer Olympics were held in Montreal. The Pisano brothers were on their way for a cross-country drive to Canada from Southern California, and when one of their group dropped out, my buddy George Pisano asked me if I wanted to go. I was invited on a Thursday, I quit my summer job that Friday, and we were on the road on Saturday morning.

My parents were hardworking people who invented the staycation experience. Because of this I had never been out of the state of California in my life. I couldn't wait to see the country! Las Vegas. The Great Salt Lake. The Sears Tower in Chicago. But especially the campus of the University of Notre Dame. We were going to be driving right by the famous Golden Dome, and my first view would be out of the tinted portal window from the rear fabric couch of the infamous George Pisano custom van.

My fascination with Notre Dame won't take too much explanation. You probably know a Notre Dame person who lives in your neighborhood or where you work. I have been one since birth; my family is part of the famous "subway alumni" of Catholics who followed the Fighting Irish football team, in no small part due to the marketing genius of its Norwegian Lutheran coach, Knute Rockne, who traveled from east to west with his teams by train in the early twentieth century, defeating all comers on the field and lashing a blow against anti-Catholicism he found at every stop.

My grandmother, born in 1896 in Missouri, was a Notre Dame fan. In the 1940s, my mom traveled to the Los Angeles Coliseum every time Notre Dame played USC, sitting in the rumble seat of her next-door neighbor's 1939 Ford. My uncle took me to my first Notre Dame game at the Coliseum in 1966 on the Saturday after Thanksgiving. The football helmets painted with real gold flakes shone on the green grass as my nine-year-old self emerged from the stadium tunnel. That was a view that is impossible to forget, as is the score: ND 51, USC 0.

What kind of Catholic would I have been without Notre Dame? During those post–Vatican II years as the Church was losing its neighborhood culture, Notre Dame continued to inspire from a distance. Notre Dame games weren't televised every week back then. I listened to the games on my transistor radio while raking the leaves on Saturday mornings. I read books about Notre Dame heroes, mostly football players, but also about its history as a mission school founded in Potawatomi Indian territory by priests from France. Notre Dame held so much mystery for me, something the Church's liturgy was losing. For my first eighteen years, Notre Dame was present only in my imagination. Now, in the summer of 1976, I was going to see the place in person.

The Pisano brothers agreed to make a quick stop off of Interstate 80 to visit Notre Dame. I remember trying to memorize each moment and sight as we turned onto campus and then got out to walk around. Notre Dame Stadium was locked, so I touched the outer walls of this sacred spot, just as I did the unique black stone in the Lourdes grotto a few minutes later. The Pisano brothers went to the bookstore to buy souvenirs, and I ducked into the side entrance of the Sacred Heart Church (now a basilica). I remember thinking how lucky I was to be there. Just a week before I had been working a mundane summer job, and now I was at Notre Dame.

My mind whirled with memories as I experienced Notre Dame with all my senses, seeing Our Lady atop the Golden Dome, my clothing drenched in Midwestern humidity. I met the Pisano brothers at the bookstore, bought some souvenirs of my own, and got back in the van.

The Olympic Games were cool—I saw the finals of the decathlon won by American Bruce Jenner. On the trip home we drove through Times Square in New York City and stopped at the Liberty Bell in Philadelphia. But there was no other feeling on that trip like sitting in the side pew on a weekday afternoon in the Sacred Heart Church on the Notre Dame campus. It was a rare spiritual moment for an eighteen-year-old, and an important one to help me maintain a shaky faith and give it the opportunity to grow in the years to come.

PLAN FOR THE FUTURE

The Grotto of Our Lady of Lourdes at the University of Notre Dame was built in 1896 using boulders—some weighing up to two tons—from local northern Indiana and southwest Michigan farms. The black stone from the original grotto in Lourdes, France, was placed on the wall under the niche of the Notre Dame grotto in 1958.

It had been collected by Fr. Joseph Maguire on a two-day stopover at Lourdes. The black stone stood out as he hiked his way up to the bluff to the site of the Lourdes grotto. He picked it up and brought it home to Notre Dame. When I began working at Notre Dame thirty years ago, I began a habit of praying the Sorrowful Mysteries of the Rosary at the grotto every Friday. I also cover my hand over that black stone just after finishing the last decade, the death of our Lord.

The original Our Lady of Lourdes grotto is located in the small town of Lourdes in southwest France, nestled along the foothills of the Pyrenees mountains. The Château Fort, a castle with origins back to the time of the Roman Empire, sits high on a hill at the entrance of seven valleys that surround the town itself. Around the French Revolution, the castle was repurposed as a prison. Today it is a museum.

Of course, the Château Fort is not the reason more than two hundred million pilgrims have come to this region since 1860, and why you might want to go there too. The *primary* destination for pilgrims is not the castle but Massabielle ("Big Rock"), a dark place at the edge of town with a grotto twenty-six feet deep and thirty-seven feet high, hewn out of the side of the mountain with a small niche protruding above. Prior to the mid-nineteenth century, residents of Lourdes usually avoided this place except to dump their trash.

This changed in 1858, when the Blessed Virgin Mary appeared eighteen times between February 11 and July 16 to a fourteen-year-old peasant girl, Bernadette Soubirous, at this grotto. On her sixteenth appearance, on March 25, Mary told Bernadette, "I am the Immaculate Conception." On the same day, Bernadette dug with her hands in the dirt and a spring of water flowed from the ground. Almost immediately, pilgrims to this site found healing in these waters. There have been more than seven thousand healings attributed to the waters of Lourdes in the years since.[1]

In 2018, a seventy-nine-year-old French nun, Sr. Bernadette Moriau, wheelchair bound since 1980, was able to walk after attending a blessing at the Lourdes shrine. "I felt a [surge of] well-being throughout my body . . . I returned to my room and there, a voice told me to 'take off your braces,'" Sr. Bernadette recalled. Hers was the seventieth Church-approved miracle to occur at Lourdes.[2]

Are you surprised that Mary would choose to appear to a poor peasant girl at a trash dump? If you study her other apparitions, you might not think so. Mary has appeared famously at other times to the poor (for example, Juan Diego at Guadalupe, Mexico) and to children (for example, Lúcia dos Santos and her cousins Francisco and Jacinta Martos at Fatima, Portugal).

Who are the people who visit Lourdes today, and how do they do it? Many choose to travel as part of a tourist package, often sponsored by their parish or diocese and accompanied by a priest who serves as guide and spiritual director. One of the largest groups that join together for an annual pilgrimage to Lourdes are soldiers from over forty countries around the world who are in need of physical, mental, or spiritual healing. The Knights of Columbus are a sponsor of this "Warriors to Lourdes" pilgrimage. You might choose a group package of some kind, or travel with your family members or even on your own.

A visit to Lourdes is high on my list of things to do in the future. I always end my Friday prayer at the Notre Dame grotto with the words St. Bernadette Soubirous (canonized by Pope Pius XI on December 8, 1933) spoke on her deathbed: "Holy Mary, Mother of God, pray for me, a poor sinner."[3] I also pray especially for those who have asked for my prayers and others who may need them.

Many years ago, when our youngest son James was diagnosed on the autism spectrum, I thought I would like to go to Lourdes with him so he could be "healed." James is in his midtwenties now, but it didn't take me all those years to realize that he didn't need mental or physical healing. His uniqueness has overwhelmed us, and I always refer to him as "the most interesting person I have ever known." Not that I wouldn't want to take James to Lourdes anyway. We, like anyone else, could use a spiritual cleansing in the healing waters of Massabielle.

ACT IN THE PRESENT

People make local pilgrimages all the time. My cross-country traveling buddy, George Pisano, gave me an idea for a really interesting walking/urban/religious pilgrimage. George was a stalworth fullback in the 1970s at Mary Star of the Sea High School in San Pedro, California. As with many football players, he had lingering injuries as he got older. After several years of immobility, George had both knees replaced. To celebrate the conclusion of his rehab, George, along with family members and friends, walked from his law office near Grand Avenue in downtown Los Angeles sixteen miles west to the end of Wilshire Boulevard in Santa Monica. The walk took almost eight hours with a few stops along the way. When the group reached their destination, not only were they on a bluff overlooking the Pacific Ocean, but also they were in Palisades Park in front of a statue of St. Monica, the patron of the city. Presumably, George and his party called on their Catholic school upbringing to offer a prayer of thanks through the intercession of St. Monica and maybe, too, through her son, St. Augustine.

I missed out on this walk but thought often about what a good idea it was and how, if I did something like this, I might make a spiritual pilgrimage out of it. I considered some of the sites I could visit if I used George's exact course from LA to Santa Monica.

For example, there are technically three cathedrals on or nearby the route: the current stunning Cathedral of Our Lady of the Angels, the former Cathedral Chapel of St. Vibiana (still open for prayer and liturgy), and the auxiliary cathedral, the massive St. Basil Catholic Church, which sits right on Wilshire Boulevard. A walking pilgrimage might include stops at each site. There is also a Catholic Charities office a block or two from MacArthur Park, a location with many homeless shelters and encampments nearby. Perhaps an hour of volunteer work could be incorporated into the urban pilgrimage.

Closer to the coast is the Church of the Good Shepherd in Beverly Hills. Frank Sinatra once attended this church. Elizabeth Taylor and Conrad Hilton were married there. This touristy information would be only a backdrop to praying a litany to the Sacred Heart of Jesus after I stepped inside. On the eastern edge of Santa Monica, there is a shrine to Mary's mother, St. Anne, at the St. Anne Church, a parish made up mainly of Mexican American families. St. Anne's could be the final stop on the pilgrimage before reaching the statue of St. Monica in the park.

If you were to plan a pilgrimage for your own region, what would it look like? Use this urban walking pilgrimage as a prototype for one of your own. Plan a course based on a distance and time you would like to walk. You might even consider making this a two- or three-day pilgrimage. If so, locate lodging at a hotel or maybe even a parish center along the way where you can stay. Choose some friends to walk with, or if you prefer for your own spiritual well-being, do it alone. Be cautious and careful.

If I ever do this exact urban walking pilgrimage in Los Angeles, I will invite all of the Pisano brothers to join in as a reunion of our 1976 Olympic Games road trip. Maybe we'll do it in 2026 for our fiftieth anniversary of traveling across the country in the infamous George Pisano van.

PRAY

> Though all the peoples walk,
>   each in the name of their own god.
> We will walk in the name of the Lord,
>   our God, forever and ever.
> In the Lord is our motivation and strength.
> May we finish our journey in his eternal home.
> We ask this in the name of Christ, our Lord.
> Amen.
>
> —based on Micah 4:5

REFLECT

- Remember a holy place you visited. Describe a sense of spiritual awakening you felt there.

- What is a holy site you would most like to visit? Why do you want to go there?

- Outline the itinerary of your own local walking pilgrimage. Map a route that includes at least three holy sites.

6

SUPPORT THE POOR

All forms of poverty, whether material poverty or poverty of the spirit, which is characterized by a malaise of hopelessness, are signs that this world is not perfect. Poverty in its various forms—material deprivation, unjust oppression, psychological illness, and death—are signs of an inherited human condition that is the direct result of original sin.

Catholic social teaching calls us to support the poor—in fact, give them a "preferential option." What does this mean? It means treating the poor with equitable care, just as a parent would give more attention to a sick child than a healthy one until the sick child had recovered. Likewise, the poor are in a vulnerable position and need our special attention. From our perspective, we should support the poor not out of a sense of duty but rather out of true love and empathy. In many ways, we must make ourselves poor, or at least poor in spirit, to make a genuine gift of ourselves to them.

REMEMBER THE PAST

This "Remember the Past" section has to be different for this experience because I've never been poor. I can share times when I participated in activities and events that were meant to assist the poor, but those occasions turned out to be mostly an opportunity for me to check off a good work for that particular Lent, summer, or year. I am certain when the activity or event was completed—the very hour after I left—the people I was there to help went right back to being poor.

Pope Francis alluded to this mindset by explaining that when we offer support for the poor, "our commitment does not consist exclusively in activities or programs or promotion and assistance; what the Holy Spirit mobilizes is not an unruly activism, but above all an attentiveness which considers the other in a certain sense as one with ourselves."[1] We need to understand that those we deem "poor" are really "rich" in the eyes of God and that we should be more like them.

For a few years, on the way to work I would drive by the same man standing on the median of a very busy left-turn lane. The long traffic light seemed to always put me right next to him. He never turned his head toward me or looked me in the eye. He held up his sign—"Hungry. Need Food. Live in a Van"—and looked off at a distance.

On one hand, I didn't really want to give him money for fear he might use it on alcohol or to feed some other addiction. So one day I decided to bring him some cans of tuna. I rolled down the window and called him over. He seemed surprised but took the tuna. The next morning on my way to work the man wasn't there, but just as the left-turn arrow turned green, I noticed the unopened cans of tuna lying out on the median.

My initial reaction was cynicism: "I knew this was just a scam to get money." But an uneasy feeling came over me, and I put some effort into thinking differently about him and what happened. My first thought was "I wouldn't eat that tuna either." In fact, it had been sitting in our pantry for months. Why would I give someone in need something I don't want myself?

My second thought was "Even if he was only looking for money, I wouldn't want to stand in the middle of the street all day with people judging me." The more I thought about it, the more I realized that this man was farther ahead of me in the line into heaven. He was the "poor in spirit" Jesus named in the first Beatitude with the addition that he is "blessed." He was Jesus himself, "one of the least ones" whom Jesus spoke about in the parable of the sheep and goats in Matthew 25:31–46. I had to either be like this man or empathize with him in a way that must become second nature.

I'm not good at that kind of thing. I know from my experiences with my own sister, who does not have as many material things as I do and who almost always has more essential expenses like heat, appliances, and plumbing that can't be paid for right when they are needed. I sometimes rationalize with "If I ever hit the lottery, I will make sure she doesn't ever have these worries again." But a gift of money to my sister isn't what's needed most. What's needed most is to listen to her stories, appreciate her pain and joys (which she has plenty of), and appreciate her presence in our family.

Pope Francis also said, "Only on the basis of this real and sincere closeness can we properly accompany the poor on their path of liberation. Only this will ensure that in every Christian community the poor feel at home. Would not this approach be the greatest and most effective presentation of the Good News of the kingdom?"[2]

Where do we go from here in our support for the poor? There are many projects and activities we can support that do, in fact, move the needle and bring aid to people in need. These are things that help to effect positive changes in large government and business structures to help attack the root problems of poverty. They also involve many options for local projects—some of them hands-on in which we can support people with needs. Whatever we do, we must lead with our attitude. We should adapt to, get to know, listen to, and love all people we interact with, especially the poor.

PLAN FOR THE FUTURE

I've recently become a member of Catholic Relief Services (CRS), a group I hope I will be able to participate in for as long as I live. You might find it engaging, exciting, and a great service just as I have. CRS is the official agency of the United States Conference of Catholic Bishops in support of the poor on an international level. It was founded at the end of World War II to provide relief to people recovering and rebuilding in war-torn areas.

CRS *chapters* are a localized effort to support advocacy for the international needs of the poor. The chapters are comprised of parishioners, diocesan groups, and other community members. A group of us at my workplace formed our own chapter. We have seven or eight people on our "core" team but also draw assistance for certain projects from the rest of our employees.

How did our chapter come about, and how might you form your own chapter? Due to the help of the CRS staff, the process was seamless. If we could do it in the midst of our workday, I'm sure you would find the formation equally doable around whatever group you choose to align with. A CRS representative walked us through orientation with about six hours of training, which was held on different days and over Zoom. The training outlined the mission, history, and operation of CRS and how a local chapter would support the goals of the international organization.

After the orientation, our chapter meets once a month and also connects a second time each month on a national conference call featuring expert speakers, questions and answers, and the introduction of core advocacy projects our chapter can work on. All of the national calls and meetings with CRS staff are taped and can be viewed by chapter members when convenient.

CRS chapters are a great way to learn about humanitarian situations in many different parts of the world and, more important, about the actions and policies that develop the capacity of local populations to own and improve these situations. A main way CRS chapters advocate for international aid for the poor is to develop relationships with local congressional representatives to encourage support for spending bills that send funding to impoverished areas. Our chapter was able to arrange two face-to-face meetings with staff members from both of our US senators. Each of these representatives came to our workplace at lunchtime. Over deli sandwiches we went around the room introducing ourselves by name and parish and explaining why advocacy for the poor around the world is important to us. Our specific topic involved encouraging the representatives to share with the senators CRS's support for reauthorization of the Farm Bill, a bipartisan congressional bill that provides flexibility and efficiency in getting training, equipment, and food for the most marginalized people in the world.

When I first became a CRS chapter member, I didn't envision myself giving pitches to representatives of elected officials. But CRS provides a bevy of information and talking points, both in written form and through instructional videos, that made *all* of my chapter members comfortable in sharing a personalized explanation for why we believe in this effort. In both cases, the representatives took copious notes on what we presented and followed up with correspondence showing how they logged our comments on the senator's website as well as personally passed on our messages to them.

Our CRS chapter also supports the poor locally. In our first year, we recruited other employees and their family members to join us on a sponsored CROP Hunger Walk, a fundraising event to fight local hunger. We set up a site for donations and had T-shirts made for our team. We all walked together from a local church about three miles to a second local church in our town, which sponsored a food pantry. We couldn't help but notice how empty the shelves of the pantry were, so we promised the pastor that we would sponsor a food donation at Christmastime. We were able to collect several needed food and toiletry products and do our small part in helping the thirty or so families who come to that pantry four times a week for assistance.

We also discovered four other CRS chapters in our diocese, including two college clubs at Notre Dame and Saint Mary's College. The other two chapters are part of parishes. We all got together for our meetings with the congressional representatives.

It was a chance to network with the other chapters and, more important, meet in person some other like-minded Catholics. One man made a point that especially resonated with me when asked why he joined his chapter: "It seemed like something beneficial and interesting I could do after I retired from my job." I agree. Being a CRS chapter member is something I can see myself getting even more involved in after I am done working full time.

ACT IN THE PRESENT

As you are no doubt aware, there are many official ways to support the poor in your local area. Food banks not only encourage donations but also welcome individuals and groups to help package and sort food, fold bags, and even write individual greeting cards to families who will be receiving the community's donations. Pregnancy centers are also in need of clothing, diapers, and formula, not to mention in-person volunteers who can help to provide hospitality to expectant and new mothers.

Consider finding out if there are local agencies in your community that help to welcome recently arrived migrants. Some of these families and individuals need entire living spaces furnished. Others are simply looking for ways to assimilate into the community. At the CROP walk we participated in, we invited three newly arrived families from Afghanistan to join us on the walk, wear our special T-shirts, and meet up at the end of the walk for punch and cookies. I could go on and list dozens of other ideas from my own community; I'm sure you could do the same for yours.

I take you back to the message of Pope Francis about how we should "connect" with the poor. The pope spoke of direct efforts to help the poor become and feel they are an essential part of society. He mentioned that the word *solidarity* when used with the poor should refer to something more than a few sporadic acts of generosity. To empathize and be one with the poor means to love the poor with an authentic love that enjoys being in their company and learning from them. St. Mother Teresa of Calcutta explained this well:

> The work we do is only our love for Jesus in action. And that action is our wholehearted and free service—the gift to the poorest of the poor—to Christ in the distressing disguise of the poor. If we pray the work, if we do it to Jesus, if we do it for Jesus, if we do it with Jesus, that's what makes us content.[3]

Because there is true joy when we love, any effort in supporting the poor must be an effort that we also love and find joy in doing.

I mentioned earlier that one of my goals is to set up a sports league for kids who don't have the opportunity to play competitive and fun games, unlike those who come from families who are able to pay for fancy tournaments and travel leagues. I like working with kids, I have experience coaching, and I love sports. So I wanted to connect something that I love and brings me joy with something that will bring love and joy to others in return.

You may find that, to accomplish this goal, you need to exercise some caution. It's important to abide by the rules, regulations, and screenings that are in place for an adult to work with kids. But these are not insurmountable challenges for someone of good character and with good intentions. I know this because I have been coaching little league baseball for the past few years. My friend had a grandson on the team and asked me to help out. The games, practices, and baseball itself were a lot of fun, but I think the biggest positive thing I provided to the boys on the team was that I wasn't a parent or a relative. I could be encouraging without any ulterior motives of "developing the next major league talent" as some parents (including me with my own kids when they were younger) often have. I saw the fruits of our work as we encouraged the confidence of the kids. It was very rewarding.

My hope is that one day I'll be able to do so with other kids who don't have the same opportunities the kids on this team did.

I know that would be an experience of love, joy, and connected-
ness with people in need that I can only dream about for now.

PRAY

> Better to be poor and walk in integrity
> than rich and crooked in one's ways.
> Rich and poor have a common bond:
> the LORD is maker of them all.
> Those who sow iniquity reap calamity,
> and the rod in anger will fail.
> The generous will be blessed,
> for they share their food with the poor.
> —Proverbs 19:1; 22:2, 8–9

REFLECT

- When was a time that you felt empathy, love, and connection with the poor?

- What is a skill and interest you can bring to the table to support those in need?

- Outline a long-term plan you have for advocating for the poor. How might participation in a Catholic Relief Services chapter align with your interests and opportunities?

7

BUILD PHYSICAL FITNESS

God created us to be an indivisible combination of our bodies and souls. Whatever we do with our bodies, we do with our souls. Most of us, at least at some point in our lives, have treated our bodies poorly. We all know that unhealthy eating patterns, tobacco use, alcohol abuse, and the misuse of other drugs all threaten our health and well-being—and that a healthy diet is a key part of the equation in treating our bodies well.

As we age, the natural wear and tear begins to take a toll, so it becomes even more important to take good care of ourselves. Our own genetic makeup and the advice of trusted medical professionals—and others close to us who care for us—can help us make better decisions in diet. The other part of the equation for bodily health is physical exercise. In this area, we have more personal freedom in choosing to do what we enjoy. We might need to adapt fitness routines we once did with vigor or choose new activities we always wanted to try but never had the time for.

REMEMBER THE PAST

There is little doubt that Christian tradition has a deep understanding of and respect for the union of body and soul. St. Augustine and St. Gregory of Nyssa, both followers of Aristotle, wrote extensively of how both the body and soul together constitute the human person. Generally speaking, the healthier our body, the healthier our soul. Yet, as far as regaining health of my own body and soul, the experience has been like a game of Whac-A-Mole . Just when I get some control of my eating habits and limiting my calories to something around two thousand a day, pride and a lack of prayer creep in. When I am more diligent on spiritual matters, I seem to find myself around the snack machine in the office, passing up the healthier "skinny" version of popcorn for a bag of corn chips.

There are two ways to physical fitness, right? Eat healthier and exercise. I have what most would deem poor eating habits. I alternately binge on certain foods for a time and then fast dramatically. This has a name—yo-yo dieting—and I am aware. Let's just say I hope to improve in the area of my diet and what is going into my body as I move forward.

Yet, with exercise, I have never stopped. Since I was a kid, I have spent most of my free time outdoors. Back then we called exercise "play," and we did it constantly. There were organized sports, running, and rudimentary weight training, but most of our exercise was in our day-to-day play.

I'll summarize in this way: About once a week, my buddy Jon and I would ride our one-gear bikes seven miles on neighborhood streets to the foot of the San Gabriel Mountains. We would then walk beside our bikes about four miles up the mountain road to Chantry Flat. Once there, we'd hike on the mountain trails for a few hours, mostly to Sturtevant Falls, where we would strip down and cool off in the water hole (and drink the water flowing from the falls). We'd dry out on the hike back up the canyon to our bikes. Then came the most fun of the day: letting loose on our bikes down the mountain until we reached Irv Noren's Market at the corner of Santa Anita Avenue and Route 66. One time at the market, a guy on a motorcycle told Jon and me, "Hey dudes, I clocked you doing 50 coming down the hill." He looked like Jack Nicholson. Whoa, in sixties parlance we were "stoked."

Keeping a sense of play mixed in with exercise has kept me motivated in all the years since. And I've noticed a new sense of adventure since I turned fifty. I'd always slogged along as a runner, keeping at about a three-mile-a-day limit and probably around eight- to nine-minute miles. In my twenties, I ran a few Saturday 10Ks—the official kind where you get a T-shirt—but hadn't done one in years. Our town sponsored an annual marathon and half-marathon, with the finish line on the field at Notre Dame Stadium. "If only," I lamented to myself. Then, one evening, just to check, I set my car's trip odometer to zero and drove on the outskirts of some running paths nearby to see just how far 13.1 miles really was. When I hit the mark, I was surprised to find it seemed doable.

The next day I set off on foot. A good thing about running alone is that there is no pressure. You can always stop. But on that day, I kept going and finished the 13.1-mile loop. I had run a half-marathon! I quickly signed up for the official event that was to take place two weeks later.

If you've done something like that, you must know how much prayer and resolve play a part. The physical pain probably set in just after the normal three miles I had been "training" at for years. The mental pain in the form of the little voice telling me to "quit" or "you've gone far enough" accompanied me for at least the last ten miles. What to do? I thought of something Bishop Thomas Paprocki—the marathon-running bishop from Springfield, Illinois—said about praying the Rosary while doing his daily runs. He spends time in prayer naming all who have asked for his prayers and offering up their personal intentions. The bishop said,

> Before beginning your run, you should have in mind an intention for which to pray, such as for someone's health, or for someone out of work to find a job, or for peace and an end to war, or for the repose of someone who has died. You can also pray for yourself, in

> atonement for your sins you have committed or in
> thanksgiving for the gifts God has provided for you.[1]

And so, as I made my way along that marathon route, mile after painful mile, I prayed all four Mysteries of the Rosary, albeit "thinking" the Hail Marys rather than mouthing them. I counted the prayers on my fingers. I used the mile markers to consider the progression Jesus made through the narrow streets of Jerusalem to Golgotha and imagined the people who had lined the race route as both disciples and enemies of Jesus. In fact, lots of the people along the route seemed to take on appearances of those roles, cheering, ignoring, or appearing to scoff as I slowly ambled by. But at last, I made it. I ran through the tunnel at Notre Dame Stadium and out to the fifty-yard line to the finish line. It was before they replaced the real grass with artificial turf, so the memory is even better. And I bounced on the runner's high for a few more weeks before looking for something else to do.

My next new adult play event turned out to be more fun than the half-marathon, and equally as satisfying when it was all done. It was a sprint triathlon held in August at Eagle Lake just over the border in southwest Michigan. "Sprint" in front of "triathlon" means the distances are manageable, unlike the original, which combines a 1.5-mile swim with a 120-mile bike ride, wrapped up by running a full 26.2-mile marathon. Cut those distances down by about 80 percent, and you have a sprint triathlon.

I prepared by swimming laps in the indoor pool at the health club until I could make one mile without stopping. I rode my hybrid bike to work and back for a few weeks, and I kept up with my three-mile runs, back at the eight- to nine-minute pace. A couple of days before the event, I took my bike into the shop for a tune-up and asked the guy there whether I should borrow someone's racing bike in order to finish the twenty-five miles a little "faster." The repair guy looked at me quizzically. "Why? Just cruise through the countryside and enjoy the view. You aren't out to win any medals." Good point.

My biggest concern was the swim. It was five hundred yards total around a buoy in the center of the lake. I knew I could make the distance, but cloudy lake water with what I imagined to be snapping turtles in the vicinity had me a little concerned. Also, some of these old people were really into this, and I didn't want to flail along and bump into them because maybe they really were trying to win medals. I stayed far to the outside on my way out to the buoy and kept my face down in the green water. Then, *oops*, I was indeed bumping somebody. But when I broke and took a look, it was actually the other person knocking into me, flailing, and looking as if the swim was not really his thing.

With new confidence, I moved toward the inner circle, flew around the middle marker, and raced the last 250 yards as fast I could. My swim time was in the top third for my age group. As predicted by the bike repairman, the hybrid bike was not going to cut it in speed, so I did sit back and enjoy the countryside. There were longhorn steers, a meandering creek, and amber waves of grain. I lifted up the Glorious Mysteries on that bike ride.

The 5K run to finish was a bit of a struggle, but there was plenty of adrenaline left to complete the event. After I got my bike loaded in my trunk, I had a sense to call my mom to tell her what I had done. I don't think she quite got where I was coming from, but I'm sure she was glad to reconnect with me on a new accomplishment of some kind.

Whatever exercise I have done in the past, what I like to do now and what I hope to do in the future has to have some element of fun. Baseball has always been my favorite sport, and not only have I been blessed to return to the diamond as a little league coach these past few years, but also, with it, I've gotten to bring my own mitt to practice, throw the ball around with the kids, shag flies in the outfield, and pitch batting practice. Pitching batting practice in your midsixties to six or seven boys who each need a bucket full of forty or fifty pitches before a game? What a workout! I finish drenched. I finish happy. I finish feeling as if I'm twelve years old again.

PLAN FOR THE FUTURE

I enjoy aerobic exercise. I don't care if the experts disagree with this choice for someone my age. It has something to do with sweat, cleaning out the toxins from my body. Just as the confessional leaves our souls cleansed, an aerobic workout has always left my body feeling the same way.

My dad was a key influence in encouraging sweat. He worked in our backyard from early morning to evening on the weekends, digging, cutting, mowing, and planting. I say "influence," but in those days he just plain made me join him in the yard work.

What a difference half a century makes. I'm still out in the yard on weekends doing some of the same type of work I was required to do as a kid. But now I enjoy it. Our yard is decent in size, but not an overly large swath of earth. Nevertheless, the different tasks of the four seasons remind me of the cycle of dying and rising, rising and dying. In April, the trees and bushes bud and I rake out the patch of space near our westernmost fence where I give a garden a new try. Pumpkins, zucchini, tomatoes, marigolds, and several other seeds have been planted over the years. In the future, I am going to do the garden up right, expand it, cultivate it with more care, and better reap its rewards.

From spring on, I pull weeds and pick up branches that fall from the trees. I trim around the sprinkler heads and climb up on a ladder to clear dead branches from the roof and keep the drain gutters clear. The dead branches remind me of my need to not be such and to remain connected with Jesus, the Vine. My dad was before his time with a mulch pile, and I constantly mix and grind in apple cores and orange peels along with clippings and dead leaves. We live on a small lake, and I have found worms love the bottom of the mulch pile, hence eliminating the need to ever purchase live bait for fishing.

Mowing the lawn is the most strenuous work I do in our yard. In the summer I mow the fast-growing grass every five days. I use a push mower, and the regular and rhythmic patterns of rows soothe a nominal case of OCD as I move through them and get them just right. Nowadays, because this weekend activity of yard work is crammed between the end of one workweek and the start of another, the process is rushed and not as mentally relaxing as I would like. In the future, when it is no longer a required chore as it was when I was a kid or a weekend time killer as it is now, I can imagine yard work reaching its penultimate status in my life. I will be able to stretch it out over days and connect with nature, dirt, and beauty while still achieving a good sweat.

I measure the quality of aerobic exercise with two criteria. The first is the number of calories it burns. Yard work with lawn mowing included takes off about five hundred calories in an hour, more than riding a stationary bike and about twice as much as swimming laps in a pool. The second criterion is how sweaty and dirty I am when completed. I love a workout where I have to peel my T-shirt off before getting in the shower, and when I then roll it up in a ball before tossing it in the washer, it feels as if it weighs ten or fifteen pounds.

"Sweat opens your pores and lets out germs and whatever else ails you." This is another thing my dad used to say, and I have no idea whether there is one shred of truth to the statement. But he believed it. He was also a big fan of running a humidifier whenever someone was sick. And when I was really young, he would press his thick, calloused hands heavily on my back while rubbing in the vaporizing cream that was meant to expel the germs and bring me back to health when I had a cold.

Can you imagine the sweat that poured forth from Jesus as he carried his Cross? We've seen the Via Dolorosa portrayed on film enough to be able to imagine a bit of what he went through. But the gospels don't mention the word *sweat* by that point in his Passion. Rather, it was in the Garden of Gethsemane before his arrest, scourging, crowning with thorns, and having his Cross thrust on him that the scriptures mention he "prayed so fervently that his sweat became like drops of blood falling on the ground" (Lk 22:44). Talk about a cleansing sweat that opened the pores of humanity to expel generations of sinfulness, past, present, and future. Jesus was anxious, the gospel says, while in the garden praying and sweating in blood. I wonder if the anxiety had dissipated during the actual path to Golgotha while the real physical strain was taking place, after the Tempter had been defeated in the final moment of prayer, and with knowledge that the power of sin was in its last hours.

ACT IN THE PRESENT

Not all exercise is or should be a solitary venture. Remember, our best times exercising when we were kids were really playing with our friends and, perhaps, playing on teams. It was that way for me. As my friend Jon and I grew up, we were more intentional in pushing ourselves and working together to get in shape. In our twenties, we would meet up around dusk and take long runs to a destination we talked about beforehand. Sometimes we would go together to our old high school and run around the track while also hoping to see some of the girls we knew exercising as well. Working out is usually more fun when done together, either with a partner or with a community of people. Working out today is a perfect activity to do with a spouse.

For many years, I've belonged to a health club. Compared to other things I usually skimp on financially, such as cable television or cell phone service, I go all out on my gym membership. My gym provides towels, a clean locker room, the requisite lap pool, other aerobic and strength equipment that allows for a variety of types of exercise, and flexible hours. Most health clubs provide all of those same things.

What I like and need most about my gym and why I go there seven days a week most times through the year is that I feel part of a community there. I mentioned I don't need in-depth conversation with most people I am around to feel comfortable, but I do appreciate the light interaction with a group of people I see regularly. In the early morning, two ladies arrive about thirty minutes before me and are just winding up their swim when I am about to get in the pool. Inevitably, one or both will motion to me between laps to let me know how many they have left so that I will know I don't have to swim my entire workout in the lane that also has the annoying steps. Their simple gesture is appreciated, and I feel connected with them in our common goal to swim back and forth.

On alternate days, I ride the stationary bike or glide on the elliptical machine near other familiar people who are consistently present. We nod, occasionally talk about the weather or the choice of music being played on the gym's speakers. I also pray the Rosary or Divine Office while on those machines. I don't recite the prayers out loud, but I do keep the phone app display of those prayers visible for the person next to me to see. I do this in humility and only with the minuscule intention that anyone who sees this might be inspired to use exercise to also pray.

Being a member of a health club means I have no excuse to skip exercise even in the most extremes of weather. It is always seventy-two degrees inside. The workouts I am doing these days help me to preserve my physical shape as it competes with the natural slide of aging so that in the future, I hope I can devote even more intentional time to the physical activities I do love. St. John Paul II touted the benefits of physical fitness and enjoyed a variety of kinds of exercise himself. "Exercise develops some of the noblest qualities and talents in people," the pope said. "Through the habit of self-discipline through long hours of exercise and fatigue we learn to take account of our own strength and how to preserve energy for the final moment when victory will depend upon a burst of speed of a last push of strength."[2]

I want to be strong in every way, to have finally flattened each mole in the Whac-A-Mole challenge of life, and to be ready for the last push of strength ahead in my final years.

PRAY

> Dear Lord, increase in me my devotion to you.
> Aid my training to be your servant.
> Perfect me in body and soul while reminding me
> that I am not one without the other.
> Keep me nourished with your words and sound
> teaching
> and focused on health of life for both the present
> and the future.
> In all toil and struggle, I am hopeful because my
> eyes are on you,
> my Savior.
>
> —based on 1 Timothy 4:6–10

REFLECT

- Keeping in mind any physical limitations, what is your ultimate fitness goal for the future?

- Name three things you found fun about exercise as a kid. How can you apply those experiences to a fitness plan today?

- Who would be an ideal partner for you in a physical fitness plan? Why?

8

CONTINUE TO WORK

Work was part of God's plan before the sin of Adam and Eve. God instructed Adam and Eve to "fill the earth and subdue it" (Gn 1:28) and "cultivate and care for" his creation (Gn 2:15) before they had sinned. Even after they sinned, work was not intended to be a punishment; the element of arduousness was added only because of the conflicts and tensions that arose among people in their work environments.

Like me, you may have found any negatives of work outweighed by many rewards. St. John Paul II said that carrying out the mandate of work reflects the very action of God the Creator, who himself worked to assemble our lives in this world. In brief, work helps us to fulfill our human destiny, to provide for ourselves, and to help others to also be able to share their gifts. I would like to do productive work for as long as I can.

REMEMBER THE PAST

"I can't get no . . ." Mick Jagger was not singing about work. In my experience, work has brought an overflowing abundance of satisfaction. I do recognize that for other people, work can be a grind, the means simply to survive and support a family. But for me, I think back to school days and closing up my geometry textbook after a night of studying and knowing that there would be no possible way to be tricked on the exam the next day because I could complete each proof backward and forward. The same would be true for a vocabulary test in English class or a quiz on how to conjugate irregular Spanish verbs. I learned early on that if I put in the necessary work of preparation—and then just a little extra besides—the rewards of labor would translate to the outcome of a good grade.

Thankfully, I always appreciated the *rewards of the work itself* and the good feeling that comes with just doing the work. My first paying job at age sixteen was to write up the football games for our high school team in the "big" daily newspaper in the area, the *Pasadena Star-News.* The process was exacting. Not only did I have to watch the game, but also I had to keep statistics like yards rushing and yards passing in real time. When the game ended I sat in my car and added all the numbers up under the light of the ceiling lamp. Then the scramble began. I had to drive to the newspaper office, climb some flights of stairs, find an unused typewriter in the office, and compose a game story, all on a hard-fast deadline and with cranky adult sportswriters throwing salty barbs my way. To this day, I can still hear myself singing to the current hits on AM Boss radio in the car on my way home well after midnight. I was happy because I had completed a challenging task.

I never appreciated having meaningful work so much as when I was without it for the first couple of years out of college. True, I was coaching youth sports part time and gaining quite a bit from the lessons I was learning, piecing together teams and from the kids themselves, but work is designed, in the best case, to bring satisfaction when it can also provide for your physical needs (housing, food, utilities, etc.) and human fulfillment (using your God-given talents). None of these things was happening for me between graduation day, 1979, and early spring 1981.

St. Monica's Elementary School needed a fifth-grade classroom teacher for the upcoming school year and, with the recommendation of my friend, Fr. Lloyd Torgerson, and the agreement of the principal and the pastor, and in a fit of desperation I am sure, I was hired as the CYO coach with little teacher training and no experience.

In the summer of 1981, I did a lot of body surfing in Hermosa Beach and tried not to think about where I would be in just a few weeks: in a classroom with a bunch of ten-year-old children and responsible for teaching them grammar, history, math, and religion. I went into overdrive a few days before the first day of school. I organized the desks and put nametags where the students would sit. I remember Cori Lamanno parking her bike, which had tassels flowing out of the handlebars, and meeting me in the doorway on my way out of the building with the message "I want to sit by the window." (I went back upstairs and moved Cori's assigned seat to the front row. She bore close monitoring, I could tell.)

I also began doing "lesson plans" in a rudimentary but detailed fashion. I was nervous about being able to fill up a fifty-minute timespan in front of forty kids and not having anything to say to them or anything for them to do.

On the first day, the entire student body lined up by grades on the pavement by the main door. Eighth graders led the flag salute and the Morning Prayer. I remember not knowing the words to the Memorare. I was still a public school kid.

Inside room 5, the feelings of meandering and lack of purpose from my previous two years dissipated immediately. I looked out over forty boys and girls and knew I was responsible for a formative year in their lives. I thought about my own fifth-grade year in school and how important it was in my development. After two years of drifting, real work had begun again. In my car on the way home after the long first day in the classroom and coaching football for two hours in the park after school (paid for only ninety minutes), I felt so grateful. I would get to do the same thing again tomorrow.

PLAN FOR THE FUTURE

In one way of thinking, there is merit to resting at the end of your life. You probably deserve it after supporting your family financially, emotionally, and spiritually for many years. But there is also a benefit in continuing to work right up until the end of your life. Jesus chose workers to travel alongside him, most notably fishermen and even a tax collector. After Jesus had commissioned his disciples to spread his Gospel and after he had specifically founded a Church on Peter, the rock, what did Jesus find after he rose from the dead? Peter and the others had returned to their previous jobs. When the risen Jesus met Peter along the seashore, Peter was just coming in from a night of fishing.

Someday I would like to return to my original profession of teaching. I've spent the past forty years or so since I was last in the classroom still in the education field, writing student and teacher materials for use in Catholic schools. In my last few years, I would like to frame my work life (as with St. Mark's gospel technique!) with a few more years of teaching. Will I be able to do it? I hope so. I did eventually acquire a teacher's credential, and with a couple of tweaks here and there, it is still valid. Advanced technology in the classroom worries me some. I am from the chalk and blackboard era. But as with most people my age who give new technology a try, I've found out that it is user friendly, not rocket science, and enhances most of what we did before in good ways.

As far as the "new generation of kids today," I would welcome the opportunity to take them through a daily theology course in a Catholic school. I am aware of the challenges. Many teens today enter their theology classes from broken family backgrounds, without any formal religious training and practice, and with bones to pick with the Church. Not all of them would be skeptics, of course, and I would rely on teens already well versed in the Catholic faith from the instruction and example they received in their homes to be of great witness to their classmates.

And yet I am sure I will learn from the doubters as well. One of the things I picked up from watching my son James, who is on the autism spectrum, go through school is that kids today are exponentially more compassionate, accepting, and welcoming than those of my generation and even the generation of students I had in class forty years ago. Yes, I would learn from them all.

I plan to give myself six months to a year of leeway in searching for a teaching job before interviewing and accepting one. I would love to have a full summer between my current job and starting to teach again. Physically, I want to be strong and able. Mentally, I want to be versed in the technology and curriculum. Spiritually, I want to examine the roster of the students in my courses before I meet them and pray for them each.

While not everyone wants to be a teacher, many of us do have a "second career" in mind. The later years of life may provide that opportunity. Social Security payments and maybe even retirement funds will be in play, as will Medicare, which can handle most of our medical expenses. So perhaps we have the wherewithal to offer a second career company an employer-friendly discount on our salary. In recent years, many jobs have gone unfilled. I also see business leaders and government officials who are much older than me doing jobs that have big ramifications and responsibilities. All this evidence gives me lots of hope for the future and putting in some productive years in the workplace for as long as it brings me joy and some worth to those I work for and with.

ACT IN THE PRESENT

Adapting my goal of employed work at a future new job may entail doing something similar as a volunteer. If there is no school out there that will hire an older man with experience to be on the faculty (and be the freshman basketball coach gratis!), then I can imagine myself volunteering in my parish as a junior high CCD teacher or catechist as part of the Confirmation preparation team, or maybe as part of RCIA as a sponsor

or instructor. Those plans would bring a lesser degree of satisfaction, to be honest, but still be worthwhile. These are also the
kind of activities I can do to practice teaching before applying
for a full-time job. They can't hurt on the résumé I will have to
dust off. I also plan to keep volunteering as a little league baseball
coach for as long as they will have me as a way to keep a sense
of the modern kid, and they of me.

After retiring from my first career, I still want to and, yes, will
probably need to make money. I look forward to some creativity
in that regard. Writing teacher and student resources both in
Catholic theology, the field I am used to, and in other subjects,
such as auto mechanics or home economics, fields I am not as
used to but do possess knowledge in the similar format of lesson
planning, are possibilities. There are also lots of online schools
popping up nationwide. I've checked their employment boards,
and there are many positions available. I don't think being an
old guy would be a detriment to being an online teacher. I might
also advertise myself as a math tutor up at least to the level of
second-year algebra. My main point is that there is plenty to look
forward to in the money-making arena in the future, and I'm not
even a businessperson. Those with a way better entrepreneurial
sense than me should be buzzing with new ideas.

All of this said, I'm aware that many people have trouble
getting jobs. Let us continue to pray for those unemployed and
underemployed so that all people have, in the words of the Second Vatican Council, "the opportunity to provide a dignified
livelihood for themselves, their families on the material, social,
cultural, and spiritual level, taking into account the role and
productivity of each, the state of the business, and the common
good" (*Gaudium et Spes*, 67).

PRAY

> I work for you with pleasure, dear God,
> not only when you watch me,

but also at all times in appreciation for the gift
of life.
All of my service to you is from my heart,
and the pleasure I receive is knowing that
my small sacrifice is a minuscule piece
contributing to the work of redemption.
Allow me to serve you all my days, dear God.

- based on Colossians 3:22–25

REFLECT

- How do you envision keeping yourself busy after retirement?

- Write up three plans for making money after age seventy
  that differ from your present occupation.

- Do you plan to work or rest in your final years? What are the
  plusses and minuses of each?

9

STAY CONNECTED WITH FRIENDS

One of the gifts of the Holy Spirit, imparted in a special way at the Sacrament of Confirmation, is the gift of knowledge. But don't think of this gift as something where the Spirit overshadows you with special abilities to understand quantum physics or to fill out the long form of your federal tax return. Rather, this gift of the Spirit is given so we might be *known* by another to the deepest core of ourselves.

Jesus knows us in this way. Unlike Old Testament heroes like Moses, Joshua, and David who were called "servants" by God, Jesus calls us "friends." He told his first disciples that "I no longer call you slaves, because a slave does not know what his master is doing. I have called you friends, because I have told you everything I have heard from my Father" (Jn 15:15). Our own friends share their lives with us as we do the same with them. Staying connected with our friends is a godly exercise. If we lose touch with our friends, we could find ourselves in danger of losing touch with who we really are.

REMEMBER THE PAST

I think back to the confluence of circumstances in my first couple of years out of college and realize that if things had gone as planned, I never would have met two of my best friends.

Mark Verge and Doug O'Neill were already best friends themselves. Mark was in seventh grade and Doug in sixth grade, and they were on my CYO teams. So I was their coach before becoming their friend. Mark says today I wasn't a very good coach at the time. For the team's first flag football game, I didn't know how many players were supposed to be on the field. I knew the number wasn't eleven, as in real football. I had a few plays on a sheet to call in the game, but Mark would wave me off. "We've got it, Coach," he would yell. And then call his own plays in the huddle.

I think Doug appreciated my coaching a bit more. He was the star of the basketball team that advanced all the way to the Los Angeles area championship game. This was well before the three-point line, and we played most of our games on outdoor courts, but Doug would rattle the chain nets from what would become the three-point distance and then lick his fingers as he peddled backward down the court. He also wore a headband.

Years of taking school way too seriously readied me for the experience of Mark and Doug. Mark flopped his way through the St. Monica's hallways with his shoes always untied and his shirt untucked. He was able to gently tease every girl without being mean. They did the same back to him. Doug was new to the school from Michigan, the youngest of four brothers. His brothers had taught him a way of the world. Doug listened to Springsteen's *The River* album on the first portable cassette player I ever saw. He spent hours at the corner convenience store dropping quarters in the Asteroids video game and shooed away anyone who tried to bother him. If I hadn't been happy-go-lucky when I was in junior high, I got a chance to appreciate the experience by watching Mark and Doug.

When my birthday came up during the school year, both guys approached me with a paper sack. "For you, Coach. Thanks for driving us to the games," Mark said while Doug nodded. The bag had $44 in ones and change. They had either collected it or fleeced it from the other kids on the team.

At the start of basketball season, Mark and Doug wanted me to ask Sr. Anne, the school's principal, if she would buy our team new uniforms. Her answer was not yes. On to plan B. The boys asked me if I would walk with them down Wilshire Boulevard after school to help them arrange sponsors for our new uniforms. Instead, I waited in my car in the middle of the block. Within an hour, they had collected enough money for new uniforms and team warmups. The school colors were green and gold, but since Mark and Doug had secured the money themselves, they rebranded the team in all black. It was only after the season that they told me the sponsors had expected their business logos to appear on the uniforms. That hadn't happened.

Mark's family lived a block over from my apartment and treated me like a member. Once in the middle of summer, his mom, Margo, caught up with me in the grocery store parking lot and invited me to come over to celebrate Mark's birthday. "Wasn't Mark's birthday in May?" I asked. Margo explained that they were just getting around to it. Every birthday in the Verge home featured Margo's spaghetti and lots of laughs around the table. Max or Lucious or one of the other many family dogs always got a plate of spaghetti too.

I would have never been able to live near Mark or the school in expensive Santa Monica if not for Doug. On overhearing a friend's parent talking about an apartment they wanted to find the "right" tenant for, Doug spoke up and said, "Coach Mike is looking for a place to live." The rent-controlled unit was my home for the next ten years, first by myself, then later with my wife, Lisa, and still later with my daughter Alex and my son Tony. We were able to live there and save money during those years, all thanks to Doug's intuition and help.

At some point in their teen years, I took Mark and Doug with me to Santa Anita race track in Arcadia to see the horses run. I had grown up near the race track, had family members who worked there in the past, and knew a buddy from high school, Jude Feld, who was a trainer there by that time. On that first visit, I "happened" to place a joint bet on an exacta for Mark and Doug, and they won. The $300 or so that they split on the winning ticket created lifelong racing fans.

In fact, Doug had no plans for college after graduating from high school. He wanted to find a job at the race track. After getting the okay from his parents, I introduced Doug to Jude, who hired Doug to clean the stables. Doug did that for a few years before getting a trainer's license himself. He's had a hall of fame career. He's been the leading trainer at the Santa Anita meet several times and is a two-time trainer of the Kentucky Derby winner.

Meanwhile, Mark's business skills went well beyond collecting birthday money for the coach in a paper bag. He was barely twenty when he opened a rare coin shop a block from St. Monica's Church. Eventually, he founded the biggest rental service in Los Angeles, assisting people in finding apartments. With the help of his wife Lani, they became real estate gurus themselves and also opened up several restaurants. Mark never lost his love for horse racing either. He bought several horses that were of course trained by Doug. And in 2010 he was hired as CEO of the Santa Anita race track. Some of the fan-friendly changes he made to the track (including free admission) are still in place today.

Mark and Doug are ten years younger than me, which looks a lot different in our sixties and fifties than it did in our twenties and teens, as does our friendship. Mark's brother, Peter, and two of Doug's brothers, Danny and Dave, all died at young ages. Mark and Doug share that bond of pain with one another, and I have been grateful to experience it with them to a smaller degree as well. Peter, Danny, and Dave are in my regular prayer intentions. I knew Danny and Dave, so it is easy to feel close to them. I never met Peter, but after I had prayed for him for many years, my dad died on the anniversary of Peter's death. I imagined my dad and Peter meeting up in heaven and discussing their common connection with Mark and me.

Mark and Doug each have wonderful families of their own now. All of their own kids are grown and successful. Doug's son Daniel works at one of Mark's restaurants. They are both practicing Catholics. I was their coach and teacher only briefly—yet we are lifetime friends. I thank God for leading me to them.

PLAN FOR THE FUTURE

St. John Bosco once said regarding friendship, "If you keep good companions, I can assure you that you will one day rejoice with the blessed in heaven."[1] I firmly believe the same thing. I'm going to enjoy the next world with my friends. We are all going to enjoy being in God's presence together.

Once again, why wait? As we lose more and more friends to death as the years go on, we have plenty of friends from our past whom we still have a chance to reconnect with, and new ones to make in the future. When I have more time, I especially want to get together in person with friends I've made throughout my life and whom I haven't seen in a number of years.

There are a few ways to do this. A group of my college friends got a good start. Though they live in different areas of the country, they plan a yearly trip to get together in various places. They've done camping in national parks and fishing trips off the coast of Baja California. They reserve one of their favorite outings for September. This is the month when college and pro football and major league baseball all have their schedule of games in progress. The guys attend three games over the same weekend. One year they went to Wrigley Field in Chicago to see the Cubs on Friday, came to visit me at Notre Dame on Saturday and watched the Irish, and then drove up to famous Lambeau Field in Green Bay on Sunday for a Packers game. They also share plenty of meals and side trips in the car and laughs during these trips.

There will also be ways to be more focused on one-to-one time with a friend. Whenever I return to California, I throw out the idea to friends that any time they want to come visit me in

Indiana, they are welcome. For a long time, no one ever took me up on it. Then, a couple of years ago Kevin Crowell, from my hometown of Temple City, told me he was coming. He stayed with us for three nights, mingling with and getting to know my family, but also getting out a bit with just me at the local casino, in a tavern to hear a classic rock band, and of course at a Notre Dame football game. We also went to Mass together. Kevin had attended St. Luke's School, so I had no qualms about insisting he go to Mass with us. It was great to spend dedicated time with an old friend. Who else but someone you've grown up with beginning in grade school can recall all the pranks, hijinks, and adventures of when we were young? I hope to follow Kevin's lead and show up for a weekend at other friends' homes when I have more time or at least stay at a nearby hotel.

I think the only rule to establish for future meetings with friends is that they have to be *in person*. Facebook and other social media are great for reconnecting with old friends, but online comments, likes, loves, and sad face emojis only go so far.

ACT IN THE PRESENT

Facebook *is* a perfect old person's social media platform. I'm glad our generation stole it from the young years ago. I've reconnected not only with old friends but also with some classmates I never really knew well and with high school alumni from classes that graduated before and after me. Facebook is a great place to share memories of growing up in the same place and at relatively the same time. There are actually special Facebook groups oriented to "old school Temple City" and likely whatever place you are from.

About ten years ago, I had an idea to bring Facebook to life. I get to Southern California a couple of times a year and thought one of those times it would be great to have a meetup with friends from the hometown Facebook page. One of our friends, a former county sheriff, had recently purchased the classic Crest Lounge in the heart of Temple City. He was happy to host what came to be called the "Big Night Out." Online invitations went out right there on Facebook. Our Big Night Out has become an annual event, with a hundred or so friends at the Crest Lounge, sitting in booths or standing in the middle of the main floor chatting about old times. A DJ plays our favorite songs, albeit at a lower volume since many of us are harder of hearing than we once were and we want to be able to converse. We've also adjusted the start time for the Big Night Out as the years have gone on. It's now more of a "Big Afternoon/Evening Out" as lots of people like to get on the road or home by 9 p.m. The days of making it to the last call are in our rearview mirror.

A few notes in case you would like to plan your own Big Night Out:

First, no nametags. Part of the fun is engaging in a few minutes of conversation before figuring out who it is that is right there in front of you. We've had a few people who like to spend at least part of the night going incognito and observing the group before deciding to interact. There's nothing wrong with that!

Second, don't let anyone make any announcements or give any speeches to the entire group. We are there for laughs and memories, not lectures!

Finally, no sit-down dinner. What's perfect about our location and format is that everyone orders their own food, or doesn't. Same with drinks. If you can find a place as cool as the Crest Lounge that also does not charge any cover to get in, then you've got a real winning location. Part of the problem with official high school reunions is that they do all of the things listed above.

By the way, there is something even simpler you can do to remain connected with your friends. Give them a phone call. Write down their birthdays on your calendar (or keep them on your digital calendar for those of you already well advanced in technology). When the date of the birthday pops up, grab your phone and share a few minutes catching up. There's probably lots to discuss from the past year—possibly some sorrowful occurrences but some joyful ones too—and always the memories.

PRAY

Lord, keep my friends and me close to you
so that we can share eternal glory together in
    your heavenly kingdom.
You have called me your friend; help me to be a
    friend to you in return.
Promise me that if you need me,
I will be loyal to you to the point of death.
                              —based on John 15:1–10

REFLECT

- Who is a friend you haven't talked to in more than five years? What is keeping you from connecting?

- What is an idea you have for an in-person meeting with friends? How can you put the idea into practice?

- Who is someone in your life that you are surprised is your friend? Why so?

10

APPRECIATE FAMILY

We don't do life alone, do we? In some way or another, we travel this road with our family members. In the words of the *Catechism of the Catholic Church*, the family is our own "privileged community," where we work out the individual course of our salvation through Christ, getting encouragement to do so from people like parents and siblings at first, and spouses, children, grandchildren, nieces, and nephews in our adult years. Sometimes our family members are related not by blood but by the love and closeness that have been cultivated with them over many years.

If the family is the foundation of society, so is marriage the foundation of the family. I especially appreciate my wife for sharing the small stuff with me day-to-day while keeping me focused on what's really important.

REMEMBER THE PAST

Have you ever wondered why your family did certain things? I do. Every Christmas was the same through my teenage years: the opening of presents in the early morning, Mass at around 9:30, a small bowl of cereal and a quick glance at our new gifts on our return, and then piling into the car for a trip to our grandmother's house. It was there we spent the rest of Christmas Day with fewer presents (which were typically clothes from my grandmother and aunt) while staying away from the commotion of the meal preparation. Our cousins were there, which was always good, but we played with them a lot on other days, and we didn't even have bikes to ride or balls and bats to play baseball. Or, if we did, it was usually rainy and cold and we had to stay inside.

After my grandmother passed away, the same format for Christmas applied except that we traveled to my aunt and uncle's house (or alternatively, they to ours). What was different is that they lived fifty miles away instead of two, as my grandmother had, and we also drove my unmarried Uncle Bill with us, so there were always three of us packed into the back seat of our Chevy Impala.

By the time we were teenagers, there were more noticeable tensions among the adults in the room. My uncles and mom used the holiday to discuss what was going to become of my grandmother's house. How were the profits of the sale going to be divided? My cousins' other grandparents were at the house too, and Uncle Bill was steamed when their grandfather gave my cousin Jim a Black Sabbath album as a Christmas gift. I learned the word *sacrilege* that day.

The television networks had begun to broadcast pro football on Christmas, giving rise to a new family custom. With my cousins, Uncle Mickey, and me sprawled in the family room watching the game, my mom kept poking her head in the doorway saying, "This is not right to have a game today. Think of all the workers at the stadium who have to be away from their families." Personally, I remember a great game between the Chiefs and the Dolphins.

Do you wonder why we did this? Put in all the effort to be together?

I got a sense of the answer after both of my parents died. They lived more than two hundred miles from the nearest relatives, yet several of my cousins came to both funerals. We had "parties" both before and after the funerals where we shared childhood memories from not only Christmas but also Thanksgiving,

Easter, and Fourth of July. Uncle Bill fretting about the Black Sabbath album got a laugh when the story was told.

My cousin Cathy talked about the lace tablecloth on my grandmother's dining room table that came out only on holidays. Sisters Kristen and Karen said they thought they would kill each other on the long drive north. But they didn't, and they even took in a wine-tasting event on the way home. I think we all realized by the end of our two days together at the funeral that the reason we put in the effort to be together then was the same reason we all put in the effort to drive five hours to be together now. The memories of those occasions were some of the most lasting we have in life. Making the effort to be together with family is always worth it.

Nowadays, we have adult children who live in New York, California, and Europe while we remain rooted in northern Indiana. Sometimes they can't all get home for Christmas. But when they do, staggering their arrivals over the course of four days until they are all under the same roof on Christmas Eve, the memories are priceless. On one Christmas Day, after Mass, one of their cousins, Megan, came over. I eventually removed myself after dinner and laid on the living room couch, letting the commotion-filled meal settle and listening to the siblings and Megan talk and laugh about Christmas memories from when they were growing up.

PLAN FOR THE FUTURE

In the years ahead I want to continue to provide chances for my nuclear and extended family to share old memories and make new ones. A basic way to do that is to continue to show up. As the sons, daughters, nieces, and nephews get older, there are engagement parties, weddings, baby showers, Baptisms, and First Communions on tap. (We pray that the sacraments will be in the future of the next generation of our family while, sadly, not taking for granted that they will.) How often have you received an invitation to one of these events and not attended because of

distance or expense or just because you didn't want to? I raise
my hand here for each of those reasons. In the future, I pledge
to change my M.O. and attend more of these events.

In the same vein, I'd like to host some larger family events
and send out the invitations to everyone—the sisters-in-law who
don't speak to one another, the estranged nieces and nephews,
and the boyfriends, girlfriends, and spouses of all. We did this
only once, when our youngest son James graduated from high
school. We put a tent canopy in the backyard, rented some extra
tables, cooked some family favorites, and had a caterer provide
the rest. We invited family from around the nation, and lots
made the effort to attend. I especially enjoyed watching James,
his siblings, and his cousins play a big Wiffle ball game at dusk
as the party was coming to an end. To host these events, I hope
to maintain our family house. I like the thought of everyone
returning to the same home base where they grew up.

Another practice to maintain is gift-giving for children in
the family under a certain age (ten? five?) on birthdays and
Christmas. These can be not only for grandkids but also grand-
nieces and grandnephews, and anyone else you count among
your extended family. The gift doesn't have to be elaborate or
expensive; in fact, a religious medal, book, or holy card with
your own personal note could be the best gift of all.

As one of the older people in the family, I will take on some
of the responsibility of preserving memories and traditions
for those in our family who will be born well after I'm gone. I
hope to write up a chronology of our family by making a photo
album that will include detailed captions and memories near
each photo. I hope I can coax one of my kids to "interview" me
and their mom in the future with any questions they have about
our own childhoods and the early years of their own lives. This
oral sharing is a wonderful way to preserve family history and
traditions for future generations.

I have a friend, Chris, who lost his son, CJ, to an aggressive
form of childhood cancer. CJ was only eleven years old. As his

sadness subsided enough to be able to offer advice and encouragement to other families, Chris posted this message to his social media: "Don't take your family for granted. Someone can be taken from you at a moment's notice. Give them a hug and tell them that you love them."

ACT IN THE PRESENT

There's no time like the present to tell people who are close to you that you love them and what you notice and appreciate about their goodness. I remember an activity from my youth minister days when I would have the teens sit in groups of five and compose short letters to each person in the group telling them what they noticed about their goodness. They had to share a specific example for each person, for example, "I saw you clean up the lunch tables without being asked" or "I like the way you button up the coat of your little sister when you meet her at the bus stop."

Why not write such notes to people in your own family? You don't have to do it all at once; maybe you can space them out to give on their birthdays. I think about what I might say to my own wife and kids:

- To James, my younger son, I appreciate your uniqueness. I *do* like to call you the "most interesting person in the world." You've had so many interests over the years: geocaching, traveling the Lincoln Highway, learning Tae Kwon Do, and so many more. Thank you for opening me up to new experiences.

- To Ellen, my younger daughter, I appreciate your laugh. I used to love hearing you giggle out loud while you were watching a television program by yourself. I've told you many times that you were born with a smile, and that's really true. Don't ever stop being happy.

- To Tony, my older son, I appreciate your kindness. You've never been mean to anyone. I remember when we competed together in a Thanksgiving father-and-son basketball free-throw contest. You made seven out of ten shots. I needed to make only three out of ten to win a turkey. I made two and was embarrassed and sad. You cheered me up on the walk home. You were only five years old.

- To Alexandra, my older daughter, I appreciate your commitment. Who would have thought when I first dropped you off at St. Aloysius School in Harlem, New York, to teach junior high math you would still be doing it fifteen years later and counting? Your dedication to your students' success and your commitment to walk to the subway, take a train, walk to school, teach, stay late to tutor, walk to the subway, take a train, and walk home five days a week amazes me.

- To Lisa, my wife, I appreciate your love. It hasn't always been easy, but through it all I never doubted that you love me. This knowledge makes the hard parts of life doable and gives me hope that your love will ready me for an eternity of the same. I see the fruits of our love in our kids, which you carried, kept healthy, and delivered. I will always be grateful and in awe.

There is no limit to how many of these notes you can write. I can think of many other things I appreciate about each person in my family. I can also write the same type of note to my in-laws, sister, nephews, and nieces—especially my niece Megan who has been part of our nuclear family from the day she was born. Practically, I can apply what I learn from each family member—uniqueness, laughter, kindness, commitment, and love—to my own actions. This is how God uses our communion with others to form us and make us ready to be with him forever.

PRAY

> Love is patient, love is kind.
> It is not jealous, is not pompous,
> it is not inflated,

it is not rude,
it does not brood over injury, and
it does not rejoice over wrongdoing
but rejoices with the truth.
It bears things,
believes all things,
hopes all things, and
endures all things.
Love never fails.

—1 Corinthians 13:4–8

REFLECT

- What is a memory you have about Christmas and the other holidays from when you were growing up?

- How have you created family memories as an adult?

- What are some other ways you will preserve family traditions?

11

CARE FOR THE SICK

Jesus didn't spend a lot of time *explaining* why people got sick. Really, the only time Jesus gave a reason for illness was after his disciples associated a man's blindness with either the man's sins or the sins of his parents. Jesus told them that neither assumption was correct. The man's blindness, Jesus said, "is so that the works of God might be made visible through him" (Jn 9:3). Then he healed the man (which, if you think about it, is a much better way to handle illness than explaining it).

While I wouldn't choose to contract a serious illness in my last years, there can be a silver lining: suffering well with a long-term sickness may be our last opportunity to let the light of faith shine through us in this world if we handle it with the right spirit and attitude. From what I've observed thus far in life, nobody chooses pain and suffering. Sickness seems to choose us—so why not be prepared if it happens to us or someone we love?

REMEMBER THE PAST

When I was in high school, I had to deliver flowers to hospitals and rest homes (one of the names for senior residences back then). I didn't like doing this, but I had no choice because my dad owned the flower shop.

Being around sick people and, worse, people who were old *and* sick creeped me out. At the San Gabriel Community Hospital, I was able to leave flower arrangements at the front desk.

A friendly candy-striper volunteer would sign off for the delivery, and I would be on my way. But the San Marino Manor was different. The person at the front desk gave me a room number, and I had to walk the flowers down the corridors until I found where they were supposed to go. I remember trying to keep my eyes focused straight ahead, but I couldn't help but peek into the rooms. Very old people in hospital gowns sat in wheelchairs or were laying in beds with eyes closed and mouths agape. When I found the room for the delivery, I would enter very quietly, place the flowers on a table, and leave before the person spoke to me—if they even could speak.

A few years later when I began to take my faith seriously, I discovered the corporal works of mercy—something I never learned in CCD. Number six on the list was to "visit the sick." I would have to do better.

My opportunity came in the summer of 1984 when my uncle Tony De Carbo had a long-term stay at the UCLA Medical Center near where I lived. My aunt Madeleine and their kids lived about fifty miles away in LA traffic and couldn't be there with him every day. I committed to visiting Tony on a regular schedule.

On the one hand, I didn't mind at all. Tony was my youngest uncle; he was only in his early forties when he found out he had leukemia. He loved sports and had been a pitcher on the 1957 USC national championship baseball team. When I was a kid, Tony would often surprise me and take me to a game. I loved my uncle.

But the cancer had taken its toll. The first afternoon I went to see him I was shocked at how much weight he had lost and how drawn his face was. Tony was a dentist; he could stand for hours all day working on his patients. Now he couldn't even get out of bed.

I tried to hide the sadness and fear, hoping I was better at it than I had been as a delivery boy wandering the halls of a convalescent home. I greeted Tony and sat back in the chair next to his bed for a visit. But I was still uncomfortable and, I believe, Tony was too. At one point he told me he planned to be back at his dental practice within two weeks. I couldn't imagine how that could be true.

Something happened to make things better. A young doctor came into the room, ready to practice his nascent bedside manner. The guy looked familiar to me, but he was the one who made the connection first. "Did you play baseball for Temple City High School?" he asked me.

"Ohhhh . . . you are the pitcher from St. Francis," I said.

We immediately went into reviewing at bats, innings, and final scores from our glory days of playing ball. Soon my uncle Tony joined in recounting experiences from his own baseball career, which was worlds better than either of ours. The young doctor and I shut up and listened to Tony. Things went from gloom and doom in the room to baseball and laughter.

Ever since that day, when I am around sick people, including people diagnosed as terminally ill, I try to remember the lesson from my uncle Tony's room at the UCLA Medical Center. Just be normal. Take away the *sick* from in front of the sick person. Talk about some of the same things you always did. Bring up happy memories. If the person is honest about the illness and what is ahead, go with the flow and ask a few questions that help him or her talk through some feelings. If not, return to the happy memories.

My uncle died just a couple of weeks after that visit. I was with him just hours before he passed. He never made it back to work, but I do think he made it home, that is, home to the baseball diamond in heaven, throwing a winning complete game.

PLAN FOR THE FUTURE

One night, well into retirement, my dad got out of bed in the middle of the night, stumbled in the hallway on the way to the bathroom, and fell. He couldn't get to his feet. Rather than disturb my mom by calling out, he lay on the cold floor for about an

hour before my mom noticed he was missing and got up to find
him. When she did, she couldn't help him get up either. They
lived in a remote area far away from me and other relatives, and
my dad insisted he didn't want my mom to call for an ambulance.

Once she was convinced he wasn't in serious danger, my
mom returned to the hallway with two pillows and a blanket.
She joined him on the floor, and they slept next to each other
there until daybreak, when they deemed it an acceptable hour
to phone the neighbor down the road to come over and help.
My dad later laughed and said, "I had a couple of the best hours
of sleep in months. It was like a campout!"

Eventually, my dad's congestive heart failure could not be
ignored, stubborn though he was. In the last eighteen months
of his life, he was in and out of the hospital, on regular kidney
dialysis, and on a slew of medications. Once, when he was taken
to the emergency room after suffering a heart attack, I heard my
mom lay into the station nurse for giving him a pill that caused
an adverse reaction when paired with his other medications.
How did my mom even know this? She didn't even have the
internet. But she was right.

Spouses have a special role caring for each other. At any age,
you might be transformed into a primary caregiver. As we get
older, the odds of that occurring increase exponentially. Have
you given any thought to how you might respond and what you
might do to get ready now? Perhaps it's time to have some general discussions with your spouse about how you will be able to
care for each other when one of you is ill. What would you do if
you were called to this role today? If your spouse is incapacitated, you must get informed about the specifics of the condition
and treatments available. While some websites are more reliable
than others, your online research can help you generate a list of
concrete questions to ask your spouse's doctors when you are
together in person at a medical appointment.

If adjustments to diet and exercise are part of the treatment plan, will you be able to help facilitate these changes with

reassurance but without nagging? To practice, work now on being more encouraging of each other with your comments and actions.

Will you be willing to accept outside help? My parents were not the best models of this. I was furious with them for not waking me up in the middle of the night when my dad fell on the floor. Though I was living far away, I would have woken up their neighbor for help—or called 911 myself. It's important to prepare ourselves to be cared for by others, even those outside of our close circles.

What if you are both ill or one or the other is unable to care for a spouse with health needs? Will your children and grandchildren be nearby? Would it be possible to live with them? Pope Francis wrote about a new vision of caring for the elderly that limits the need for care facilities in his encyclical *Fratelli Tutti* (*All Brothers*) saying that every effort must be made to enable the elderly to live in a "family" environment during this phase of life. "We fail to realize that, by isolating the elderly and leaving them in the care of others without the closeness and concern of family members, we disfigure and impoverish the family itself," the pope wrote.[1] Pope Francis is right; the benefits of such a multigenerational living arrangement would benefit everyone, especially grandchildren and grandparents.

Nevertheless, I want to be ready with a backup plan. Our four children live on the East Coast, on the West Coast, in the Midwest, and in Europe. Would they really be able to take us in? Would we really want to go where they are?

I recently took a look at a retirement home located on the property of the motherhouse of the Poor Handmaids of Jesus Christ, a religious community with German roots that settled near a lake and amid farmland in Donaldson, Indiana. They offer individual apartments with lake and country views. They sponsor a retreat center and junior college on the same property, and there is hospital care nearby along with an invitation to study at the college and use its gym facilities. A Catholic priest lives on the premises and celebrates daily Mass in the beautiful motherhouse chapel.

There could be worse places to live. While I'd rather live with my kids and (future) grandkids, or remain in my own home, life has a way of intervening. Having options is a good idea. It's better to be prepared.

Also, are you familiar with the term *palliative care*? This refers to medical treatment that is focused on managing pain rather than curing a condition. It is holistic in that besides using medicine to control symptoms of sickness, it focuses on the psychological, emotional, spiritual, and social factors that affect a sick person's well-being.

Palliative care recognizes the dignity of the sick person *while they are living*. This approach, used by many reputable hospice programs, should not be confused with "dignity in dying," a popular euphemism for euthanasia or assisted suicide, which is against Church teaching. Creating an advance directive (sometimes called a "living will"), a simple legal document that indicates what medical interventions you do or do not want in the event you are incapacitated, offers a good measure of security and protection against other people making medical decisions for you.

All life is valuable, and it's important not to give in to the mentality that is focused on easing death while not valuing life. When sickness wears on a person, it can be tempting to devalue this gift. When you hear an older person or a sick person say, "I don't want to be a burden on anyone," it's important to reassure them. Life is not a burden but a blessing.

Visiting the sick is a public and personal way to affirm the value of every life. As you begin to have more time on your hands, perhaps you (and your spouse) can participate through your parish in visiting the sick and homebound. What does this entail? Usually this involves a short training session where you will be given some tips for being comfortable around a sick person, what to talk about, how to pray together, awareness of the person's condition, and instruction in the rite for bringing Holy Communion to the sick, which would be part of your visits. Whether you are caring for your spouse or meeting someone for the first time, bringing Jesus to them and being Jesus for them is the best gift you can offer.

ACT IN THE PRESENT

Contrary to the popular secular view, for Christians, sickness and suffering have meaning and purpose in that they allow us to share in the same experience of Christ, who suffered not only a brutally painful death but also the emotional, mental, and spiritual pain of his Passion.

We don't have to go to heroic means to accept sickness and suffering. Our dignity and worth are not dependent on that. In a more basic way, sickness and suffering allow us to practice our dependence on others. For those who visit with us and care for us, our sickness allows them to be more virtuous. The same is true in reverse.

Would I want someone to visit me when I am sick for a duration? I think so, but maybe not all of the time. I say that because my mom was like that in her last few years. I would ask her if she wanted me to bring some of my friends along when I went to visit her, and she would always tell me no. She knew and liked these people, but she didn't want to see them. She was hard of hearing and immobile, and she had shrunk in size from when these friends last saw her. I think she didn't want them to see her that way. However, most people who are sick and homebound (or convalescing) do like visitors.

I actually have done a complete about-face from my early years as a flower delivery guy; I don't mind visiting with a sick or hospitalized person. The older you get, the more practice you get. Drawing from my experience with my Uncle Tony, I enjoy reminiscing with people who are laid up in bed or their easy chair about things we have in common or interesting details about their lives that I never knew. Sharing memories makes history come to life.

I'm still sometimes uncomfortable with a sick person's physical appearance, so I've learned to look the person right in the eye when I am talking. Also, I avoid drawing others in the room (e.g., doctors, nurses, or relatives) into our conversation. I'm sure the sick person gets enough of people translating their words and wishes. Personally, I don't mind topics of some depth, including spiritual things. But I'm aware of when I need to slow down that line of conversation and not pretend to have answers for deep questions like "Why am I suffering?" I also respect the person's time. At the first sign of weariness, I excuse myself while promising to return on another day.

If they are willing, I sometimes like to record conversations of those in palliative care. I want to hear their entire life story in as much detail as possible. What do they remember about their childhood? Where did they meet their spouse? What career did they have? I also want to ask them about their Catholic faith. What do they remember about growing up Catholic? When did they come to know Jesus? What do they like about the Church now? What do they miss about how the Church was then? Again, if they are agreeable, I write up the conversation in narrative form and give them the option of having their written life story bound in a printed book. This is a service that matches my own skills and is something I enjoy doing.

Encouraging the sick by talking about the benefits of uniting our sufferings with the Passion of Christ, and offering it up for the benefit of others, is another distinctly Catholic way of bringing dignity to their current situation. St. John Paul II wrote that "our natural aversion to death and this incipient hope of immortality are illumined and brought to fulfilment by Christian faith, which both promises and offers a share in the victory of the Risen Christ" (*Evangelium Vitae*, 67).

Watching my mom in her last months was difficult because I don't think she ever understood the connection between her suffering and Christ's suffering. While I tried to help her, obviously she needed to hear this message from someone else. She had been a kindergarten teacher for forty-five years. She missed being able to drive her own car to school, walk into her classroom, play the piano for her students, and lead them to the bus at the end of the day. Her body was failing her, and she had trouble understanding how her life had any meaning left without being able to do the things she had done in the past. So I used those memories as a way to connect with my mom in her final months, talking about how her grandkids were doing with their jobs, who they were dating, and the prospects for the Notre Dame football season. Perhaps she would have appreciated getting into deeper spiritual topics with a person whom she didn't know well, or maybe even at all. We all have a role to play in fulfilling the corporal work of mercy to visit the sick.

PRAY

> Dear Lady, Mother of Suffering,
> we remember the crosses of pain you bore in
>   raising Jesus and
> watching him die.
> Be our support as we face our own suffering and
>   witness
> the suffering
> of those we love.
> Help us to unite our cross with the cross of your
>   Son.
> Help us to bring comfort to those who are
>   anxious
> and who dread their illness
> so they might discover meaning that brings them
>   to your side in heaven.
> We ask this in the name of our Savior, your Son,
>   Jesus Christ.
> Amen.

REFLECT

- Describe your comfort level in visiting the sick. What steps can you take to feel more comfortable around the sick?

- What plans do you have in place if you, your spouse, or another family member you care for has a long-term illness?

- Picture yourself suffering a long-term illness. How will you convey to others that you find meaning in your suffering by connecting your illness with the Cross of Christ?

12

CHANGE YOUR LIFE

The rich man in the parable with Lazarus (see Luke 16:19–31) desired mercy. Caught in the chasm between heaven and hell, he begged for a cool sip of water from the poor man who sat at the side of Father Abraham. But it was too late. The rich man had numerous chances to care for poor Lazarus while they were alive but had ignored him. Even the rich man's request to warn his family about the fate they would receive if they likewise ignored the poor was dismissed.

Do you worry about being like the rich man in this parable? I do. Though I have not literally shut the door on a starving man with open sores crouched on my porch, I have ignored the poor in other ways. I have been dismissive of those the Old Testament describes in a Hebrew word, *anawim*, which means "poor people who remain faithful in difficulty." Anawim are the "poor in spirit" of the Beatitudes who, despite being ignored and stepped over, continue to remain positive, joyful, and dependent on God.

The anawim will be central characters in heaven, and they demand the attention of those of us who are rich and haughty in our ways right now. When we were younger, we were easily able to be remolded like soft clay. We are now hardened, but not completely so. We, unlike the rich man, still have time to change.

REMEMBER THE PAST

I sometimes imagine my own "Judgment Day" to be initially set in a movie theater—not a 1960s-style theater with imitation velvet seats caked with stale Jujubes beans but one of these twenty-first-century theaters with the comfy leather recliners that sink you into softness. As I envision it, I am completely alone in the theater. In fact, the rest of the auditorium is so dark I wouldn't be able to see another person even if he or she was sitting right next to me.

The screen is magnificent. It is actually multiple screens in the round, like the old "America the Beautiful" show at Disneyland. The movie begins, and I immediately recognize that it is going to be a period piece, set in the late 1950s according to the models of cars that are in view. I see a two-toned Chevy Nomad station wagon and a man walking toward it. There is a woman too, being pushed in a wheelchair and holding a baby. When they arrive at the car, I recognize the man as my dad and the woman as my mom. The baby must be me.

From there, I watch my life on film. The production quality is like nothing I have ever seen. Cameras seem to record from all angles. My parents would have won multiple Oscars for their performances. As I grow and begin to get out and about, I look pretty good on-screen myself. The film doesn't include every waking minute of each day—rather only interesting scenes that seem to have some meaning. I see the struggle I had in learning to tie my shoes and the joy when I was finally able to do so. I watch my parents reward me for this accomplishment: my first baseball glove. Ah, yes, that's where my love for baseball began!

The scenes on the screen move on and settle on my fifth-grade year in school. I look forward to what will be shown in this episode. I loved my teacher, Miss Seidler. As I am thinking this, the dim lighting in the theater rises. I peek behind me and see the figure of a woman. It seems to be Miss Seidler, but I am not sure. She has a serious expression. Near her is a boy wearing glasses and a T-shirt with an image of the 1964 World's Fair. Who is he? I get a queasy feeling.

On the screen I see the basketball courts at Cloverly School. I recognize Keith, Leo, Jim, some of my other friends, and Coach McClelland. The camera pans to the sidelines and moves in for a closeup. It is me and the boy wearing glasses and the World's Fair shirt. "Go away! We don't want you on the team!" The voice is mine. The film then switches to black and white. I am not watching my life story anymore; I am watching the life of the boy with glasses. I remember now. His name is John Homan.

I see John in a kitchen with his own mother. He is crying. His mother comforts him. He is still wearing the World's Fair shirt. This is the aftermath of me telling John Homan I didn't want him on our team.

I feel awful about what I am watching. I want the film to stop. I want to get out of my cushiony chair and go to where John Homan is sitting in the theater and apologize for what I said to him on the basketball court in 1968. I am not sure if I will be able to.

When I imagine Judgment Day in this way, I keep in mind that there will be a Just Judge present. There will be no cries of "that's not fair!" My actions will judge themselves. Jesus, the masterful film editor, will be there to fast-forward the film to show me how I changed my life after my cruelty to John Homan. What did I do to make amends and do better? And where I still came up lacking? Jesus, the Just Judge, will be there with his mercy.

PLAN FOR THE FUTURE

We don't have to wait until we've died to review the poor and sinful behaviors we've made in life, and address them directly with the people we have hurt. We can begin now to directly make amends to those we have hurt.

Making amends is different than saying a forced "I am sorry." It is even different from receiving the Sacrament of Reconciliation, when you confess sorrow, receive absolution, and do some form of penance. When you make amends, you actually show someone how you have changed and become a different person from when you hurt or injured them.

In twelve-step recovery programs, steps eight and nine involve making amends. In step eight, you make a list of all the people you have harmed and cultivate a willingness to change. Step nine involves directly making amends to those people, if possible, unless your actions would do greater harm. For example, sometimes those with alcohol or drug addictions steal money from other people. The making of direct amends involves not only repaying what was stolen but also proof of change in attitude and in life.

Very often we can't directly make amends to those we harmed years ago. However, we can and should ask God for opportunities to indirectly make amends in all cases. If we look closely, God will provide us with the chances. I think back to my years of coaching CYO sports and teaching junior high school. I was naturally drawn to looking out for kids who were picked on or who did not get a chance to be on a team. Perhaps subconsciously, I was trying to make amends for how I treated John Homan in fifth grade. One season, rather than cut a couple of boys from the basketball team, I convinced the school principal to sponsor a "B" team so that everyone would have a chance to play.

Who are the anawim—the poor and vulnerable ones—God has put on your heart to directly or indirectly make amends for the past? The opportunities are endless: children in foster care, children with special needs, children or adults with emotional or mental challenges, migrants without a home, people displaced from a previous home, children or adults who are lonely, and many more.

Sometimes my indirect amends may take the form of making a monetary donation to an organization already helping particular anawim. I hope I'll be able to also devote my own time and actions to directly working with people like this to indirectly make amends for someone similar whom I may have hurt in the past.

Will there be opportunities for making direct amends in the future too? Sure there will, especially in our age of social media and internet searches. With a few clicks, we can reconnect with all kinds of people from the past. It affords the opportunity to offer a well-worded letter or an internet message to someone I've offended. We can say something simple like: "You know, I remember we were once great friends. I'm not sure what caused us to get mad at each other and go our separate ways, but I hope we can be friends and remember all the good times we once shared."

The goal for this type of behavior is not to balance scales between a record of doing bad and doing good. Rather, it is to reform your life and become as a new person. St. Paul is the prototype for change in the New Testament. We first meet him as a strident law-obsessed Pharisee who holds the cloaks of those who throw stones to kill St. Stephen, the first Christian martyr. Paul is then blinded by the light of Christ and becomes an apostle of the faith, a great missionary and theologian, and eventually a martyr. Quoting his words in the letter to the Romans, Paul had "put on the Lord Jesus Christ" and made no provisions for anything else (Rom 13:14). He had undergone *metanoia*, a Greek word for conversion, changing his mind and heart from one point of view to another. Metanoia is an act of faith, not something we can do on our own. Pope Benedict XVI explained that St. Paul's metanoia "came from the outside: it was not the fruit of his thought but of his encounter with Jesus Christ."[1] Our own metanoia is one that can be accomplished only through the grace of God, but jump-started by our willingness to pray, repent, amend, and do good works. We prepare ourselves for eventually meeting Christ, the Just Judge, by taking on his mind, thinking like him, and loving like him.

ACT IN THE PRESENT

Those in twelve-step programs are required to make a list of all
the people they have harmed and to be willing to make amends
to them all. Sponsors recommend strongly that those completing
this step make this list in writing and, in some cases, incorporate
this step into regular journal writing. Each part of this step has
a counterpart in our Catholic practice and is something we can
do on an ongoing basis.

First, we can regularly examine our conscience. This is something we should do nightly, just before going to sleep, as part of
a review of our day to see where we may have slipped up and
treated someone unfairly, rudely, or downright meanly. These
could be people we live with, work with, interact with in the
community, or drive next to on the road. There are several formal examinations of conscience recommended by the Church
before going to Confession that can also help us to recall people
we have offended both in the past and more recently. Recalling
Jesus's command to "love one another as I love you" (Jn 15:12),
we can ask ourselves questions such as these:

- Do I treat people with the respect with which I wish to be
  treated?

- Do I contribute to the well-being and happiness of others?

- Do I help those in need?

- Have I hurt another person either physically or emotionally?

- Have I refused to help a person in need?

- Have I tried to force others to do things my way?

- Have I allowed jealousy to ruin a relationship?

- Have I encouraged others to sin either actively or by my
  silence?

- Have I gone against my conscience?

Metanoia is also accompanied by growth in the virtues.
Human virtues govern our actions, help us to control our

passions, and guide our actions by faith and reason. We can acquire human virtues through repeated efforts of good actions. The source of all human virtues is the God-given cardinal virtues of prudence, justice, fortitude, and temperance. These guide our intellect and will and help us to live moral lives.

Second, consider keeping a journal. Accompanying a regular examination of conscience with writing is also a very Christian practice. There are several methods of Christian journal writing, including writing your own meditations on the daily scripture readings or writing your own prayerful meditations.

A recommendation for journal writing to help you to facilitate a change in your life and put on the mind of Christ is that you direct your writings to Jesus himself. In the hope of drawing closer to Christ, how about beginning at least every few days of your journal entries with "Dear Jesus" and then writing directly to him about things that are on your mind and what may be troubling your conscience. St. Paul also wrote that those of us who have heard of Christ, know him, and were taught in him should "put away the old self" of our former ways of life "and put on the new self, created in God's way in righteousness and holiness of truth" (Eph 4:22, 24).

PRAY

> Lord, make me more like you.
> Allow me to seek you now while you may be
>   found,
>   call on you now while you are near.
> Reform me from my wicked ways
>   and my sinful thoughts.
> Make your ways my ways.
> For as the heavens are higher than the earth,
>   so are your ways higher than my ways
>   and your thoughts higher than my thoughts.
>   —based on Isaiah 55:6–9

REFLECT

- How do you imagine you will be confronted with your past sins and errors on Judgment Day?

- What is something new and good about you now as compared to your past?

- Name three other ways you would like to be more like Christ.

13

DRAW CLOSE TO THE BLESSED MOTHER

Devotion to the Blessed Virgin Mary is a distinctive part of being Catholic, right? If you look closely, you will find a reminder of Mary nearby, maybe in a statue in front of a church or on a neighbor's front lawn. You might be able to sing a song to Mary by heart. Her distinctive "Marian blue" seems to be everywhere. What are your memories of Mary? How are you devoted to her?

According to St. Maximillian Kolbe, a martyr at the hands of the Nazis, grace flows from the Father to the Son and through the Holy Spirit and Mary to humanity. However, Kolbe also said that the human reaction to this grace flows in the inverse direction: to Mary first and then the Son and Father by way of the Holy Spirit. This places Mary first in line to hear our pleadings and advocate for us to God as she did for us when we were children, does for us now, and will do at the hour of our death.

REMEMBER THE PAST

Taking swimming lessons with Kenny Farr, my first friend in our neighborhood, at the high school pool in the summer before going into first grade is not among my favorite childhood memories. There seemed to be a hundred of us little kids holding on for dear life to the wall of the Olympic-sized pool. Our instructors were teenage boys wearing red swim trunks and perched high above us on both sides of the pool in lifeguard stands. These weren't the laid-back post-Beatles British Invasion American teens. Our instructors had marine crewcuts along with whistles and megaphones. They screamed their messages: "Kick your feet! Faster, kid! No stopping!" Oh, and the water was freezing too.

But this was small-town America in 1962, and neither Kenny's mom nor my mom was waiting by the pool with a smile and a towel. When my mom asked me how swimming lessons went, I just nodded. I did the same thing after the second day when a red-trunked sixteen-year-old ordered me to push out from the wall and swim out to him a few feet away. Did he forget that I didn't know how to swim? It was going to be a long two weeks.

But on the third day, I didn't go to the high school pool. I thought I was headed there again; I had my swimsuit and dour look on in the car. My mom kept driving north past the high school, past the Huntington Drive intersection, and onto a shaded street near the local arboretum where peacocks lived and sometimes flew into the neighborhood and sat on the roofs of the fancy houses. We got out of the car, and I remember walking along a brick path with pine needles in the crevices that crept up between my toes in my sandals. Even before we reached the side gate, I could smell the chlorine. And there it was: a kidney-shaped backyard pool. My new swim teacher was sitting on the diving board with tanned legs hanging over the edge. Her name was Sue. She was nice. I learned how to swim the length of the pool by the end of the week.

The unanswered question at the time was "How did my mom know?" How did she know that the swimming lessons at the high school pool were not only ineffective but also very scary? And how did she find this house on a shady street with a pool and Sue? What I *did* know at age five was that I trusted my mom. I felt secure with her and knew she was the most important person in my life.

Time goes on, of course, and a kid's relationship with his mom changes. But even in the ornery teen years when my communication with my mom was sometimes reduced to grunts and groans, I continued to depend on her and live my life outside the family home as if she was always watching. I did not want to disappoint my mom. I loved my mom, and I knew for sure that she loved me too.

I feel the same way about God's Mother, Mary, that I did about my own mom. My connection with Mary certainly has a lot to do with my own mom's devotion to her. I also remember a priest at a Catholic summer camp telling us boys, "When we say a Hail Mary, it makes our Blessed Mother feel good." More than a half century later, I like to throw out a few Hail Marys during the course of a day if only for that purpose. I think about Mary a lot, and I can feel her with me as I once could sense my own mom's presence even if she wasn't in the same space. I think of the perfection of Mary as the highest of all of God's creatures. She is Queen of even the angels. She was also created just like us, and she never sinned, never wavered, and always had her life in tune with God's will. Life would be easier, it seems, if I could do that.

I imagine Mary in different ways, none of them really looking like an icon on a church wall. I think of her like my mom (also named Mary). The Blessed Mother is a woman of action. She recognizes when things aren't right, like at the high school swimming pool, and provides new and better opportunities. I think of her like Sue, the tanned teenage girl I knew when I was five, confident and beautiful. I think of her like Sandra Valdivia, the fifth-grade girl with the skinned-up knees and sweaty hair from my first year at St. Monica's—tough and independent. I think of Mary of Nazareth as a Jewish teenager who said, "Let it be done according to God's will" not just once, to the angel Gabriel, but every day of her life on earth and every day since from her throne in heaven.

PLAN FOR THE FUTURE

"God's got this." You may have heard someone say this when either they or someone close to them is facing a difficult challenge, such as a life-threatening illness. What they mean is that the situation is in God's hands, not the person's own hands or the relative's hands or the doctor's hands, but God's hands.

Sometimes "God's got this" seems like a throwaway phrase or words of last resort, but the phrase is really true. God's providence does direct our entire lives and the lives of everyone who has ever lived. God has a masterful plan; he knows how it ends, and it ends well. God's providence "spans the world from end to end mightily and governs all things well" (Ws 8:1).

God's providence doesn't diminish our free will. We still have free choices to make along the way that can affect our place in God's plan, but God is above our choices, watching them unfold, and hoping our free choices keep us on the course to him. I like to think of this as a trail of ants on their way to a Popsicle that is melting on the sidewalk. Some of the ants are already enjoying this treat. Other ants are many feet away at the beginning of their journey. Still other ants have veered off or are heading in a completely opposite way, and it doesn't look as if they will ever reach the Popsicle. From our perch way above, we are watching this all unfold. Maybe, for fun, we place a blade of grass in the way of the ants going the wrong way, hoping they will turn around. We watch this entire trail of ants, beginning to end, happening right now on our terms. But in "ant time" and "ant space," this journey is over many miles and days. For God, our lives and all of history are likewise happening right now at the same time. He is watching and sometimes redirecting us in the hope that we reach the place where we are supposed to be—with him.

When Mary answered the angel Gabriel with her *fiat*, "I am the handmaid of the Lord. May it be done to me according to your word" (Lk 1:38), she recognized that this moment was for her own glory, but Jesuit Jean Pierre de Caussade writes, in *Abandonment to Divine Providence*, "the magnificence of this glory would have made no impression on her if she had not seen in it the fulfillment of the will of God."[1]

Mary's complete answer of yes to God via the angel Gabriel was a yes to align herself with the will of God. This seems an impossible task for us if not for a simple way: to consecrate ourselves to Mary and to allow her to completely direct our wills to God through her Son. Consecrating ourselves to Mary means giving Mary permission to conform us to the will of God.

How can she do this? St. Maximilian Kolbe, who gave his life in place of another prisoner at Auschwitz, found the answer in Mary's title of "Immaculate Conception." The title refers to Mary being conceived in her mother's womb without original sin. Mary's Immaculate Conception does not make her God, but it does make her like God in a very important way. She, according to Kolbe, is the "created Immaculate Conception" in the same way the Holy Spirit, the Third Person of the Holy Trinity, is the "uncreated Immaculate Conception."[2] The Holy Spirit is conceived from the love between God the Father and God the Son. Mary is so closely connected with the will of God that God listens closely to her words and prayers. Jesus acquiesced to his Mother and performed his first miracle at the wedding at Cana, changing water to wine. In consecrating ourselves to Mary, the created Immaculate Conception, we allow her to direct our will to God because the Holy Spirit lives completely in her.

You may wish to consecrate yourself to Mary in the future but wonder how to do it. In one way, the action is simple: you make a promise to Mary to allow her to fulfill her motherly task and conform you to Christ. But before you make that promise, realize what it entails. It means giving Mary permission to take your prayers and good actions and distribute them where they are most needed. Maybe there is a child facing a difficult surgery somewhere in the world whom you don't know about and Mary would like to apply your prayers to that child's needs. The good news is that you no longer have to worry about praying by name for a particular person or particular intention, though you can certainly still do that if you wish.

Before consecrating yourself to Mary, you may want to take part in a personal and simple retreat. I began my retreat thirty-three days before the Feast of the Immaculate Conception. I spent about thirty minutes on each of those days reading and praying. The thirty-three-day period was originally suggested by St. Louis de Montfort as a way to free ourselves from our own will and the ways of the world before giving over everything to Mary. You can make a thirty-three-day retreat at any point during a year, but it is recommended that you choose an end point on a Marian feast. De Montfort offers his own writings to facilitate a preparatory retreat before making formal consecration. There are many other abridged retreat plans available today as well.

When I made my formal consecration, I did so using these words of Kolbe:

> O Immaculata, Queen of Heaven and earth, refuge of sinners and our most loving Mother, God has willed to entrust the entire order of mercy to you. I, (name), a repentant sinner, cast myself at your feet humbly imploring you to take me with all that I am and have, wholly to yourself as your possession and property. Please make of me, of all my powers of soul and body, of my whole life, death and eternity, whatever most pleases you.
>
> If it pleases you, use all that I am and have without reserve, wholly to accomplish what was said of you: "She will crush your head," and, "You alone have destroyed all heresies in the world." Let me be a fit instrument in your immaculate and merciful hands for introducing and increasing your glory to the maximum in all the many strayed and indifferent souls, and thus help extend as far as possible the blessed kingdom of the most Sacred Heart of Jesus. For wherever you enter, you obtain the grace of conversion

and growth in holiness, since it is through your hands that all graces come to us from the most Sacred Heart of Jesus.

V. Allow me to praise you, O sacred Virgin.

R. Give me strength against your enemies.[3]

Have I lived out my promises to Mary perfectly since consecrating myself to her? Of course not. But I have tried by saying a shorter consecration renewal prayer every day.

I also joined the Knights of the Immaculata, a society founded by Kolbe, with the intention of spreading Marian devotion to all corners of the world. I wear a Miraculous Medal around my neck and a chain on my wrist to remind me that I am chained to Mary, my Mother, in all my words and actions. During each day, I say to myself, "I desire to fulfill your will, Immaculata," knowing that her will is the embodiment of the will of the Father, Son, and Holy Spirit. I have also tried to make it a habit either at Lent or Advent each year ever since my formal consecration to renew my consecration promises to Mary after making another personal retreat to draw closer to her and the fullness of her grace. In the future, I hope to increase my devotion and dependence on Mary, my Mother.

ACT IN THE PRESENT

Before Notre Dame played Miami University in football in 1988, an uppity team chaplain for Miami (a Catholic priest) told Notre Dame coach Lou Holtz to remember that "God doesn't care who wins the game." Holtz responded, "I agree Father. God *doesn't* care who wins the football game. But his Mother does."

Like Coach Holtz, I have found that Mary loves football, particularly Notre Dame football, and may have even taken a hand in a few outcomes. In 1980, Notre Dame kicker Harry Oliver lined up for a fifty-one-yard field goal against Michigan with Notre Dame trailing 27–26. Just before the kick, a gusty wind that had been swirling throughout the game suddenly died down. Oliver's kick sailed through the uprights just as time expired, and Notre Dame won the game 29–27.

Ever since the priest at summer camp told me that hearing a Hail Mary makes Mary feel good, I have said plenty of them. She does seem to like them. Every morning, either in the car on the way to work or at the gym on the treadmill, I pray five decades of one of the Mysteries of the Rosary: Joyful Mysteries on Mondays and Saturdays, Sorrowful Mysteries on Tuesdays and Fridays, Luminous Mysteries on Thursdays, and Glorious Mysteries on Sundays and Wednesdays. Saints in every age have told of the benefits of praying the Rosary. De Monfort said that if we pray a daily Rosary, "I do assure you that, in spite of the gravity of your sins, you shall receive a never-fading crown of glory."[4]

As you likely know, the recitation of Hail Marys, Our Fathers, and Glory Bes is not the source of our meditation when we pray the Rosary. In the Mysteries of the Rosary, we take a trip through the life of Christ and the victory of salvation he has won for us in his Passion, Death, and Resurrection. The graces we hope to receive from our daily praying of the Rosary are to be able to imitate its Mysteries and obtain its promises.

Personally, I am overwhelmed with gratitude for the graces Mary has secured for me in both my career (I work at a company named "Hail Mary" in Latin) and especially my family life. During football Saturdays at Notre Dame Stadium—win or lose—because I am the field supervisor, I stand at the fifty-yard line as the stadium empties, thanking her, praising her, and loving her for her goodness to me.

PRAY

Away from us Satan.
On your belly you shall crawl,
    and dust you shall eat
    all the days of your life.
A woman clothed with the sun
    with the moon under her feet

and a crown of twelve stars on her head
will strike at Satan's head
and crush him.
She will bring us to her Son, our Lord.
Amen.
—based on Genesis 3:14–15 and Revelation
12:1–2

REFLECT

- What are your memories of your devotion to Mary?

- Identify some graces Mary has provided to you in your life.

- What is a Marian feast day that you would choose for consecrating yourself to the Blessed Mother? Why is this day special for you?

14

PREPARE TO BE A SAINT

When Thomas Merton, the twentieth-century spiritual writer, was asked by his friend, Lax, what he wanted to be, Merton responded, "I don't know. I guess I want to be a good Catholic." Lax shook his head. "What you should say is that you want to be a saint."

Merton brushed him off. "How do you expect me to become a saint?"

Lax answered, "All that is necessary to be a saint is to want to be one. Don't you believe God will make you what he created you to be, if you consent to let him do it? All you have to do is desire it."[1]

For any of us who are going to heaven, there will be no escaping the title *saint*. That is what we will be. More, if we live a heroic, virtuous, Christian life in this world, we can already claim the title *saint*. Fourth-century bishop Nicetas asked succinctly, "What is the Church if not the assembly of all saints?" (*CCC* 946). All that is necessary to be a saint is to want to be one.

REMEMBER THE PAST

Let's clarify: in saying we want to be saints, we are talking about saints with the lowercase *s*, not advocating for a canonization process here on earth to begin after our deaths to determine our title with the capital *S*. Of course, we are still eligible to be a canonized saint, but that is not something we should advocate for. Personally, I expect that if I am a saint, that means I'll eventually be in heaven and in the presence of my family and friends who are also saints, and Mary, Jesus, and all the big *S* saints too. That goal's enough for me.

How to become a saint? Incorporating the virtues into our lives so they are second nature is a surefire way. In thinking back, I notice that the times I exhibited the most faith and practiced the most virtue (for example, humility and patience) are when I lost something or chose to give up something that was important to me. I think the reason I noticed a growth in faith on such occasions is because of the grace that seems to accompany these times.

One example from my own life goes back many years. I was almost sixteen and playing the last game of the season in a summer baseball league. I lived for baseball, had been a little league star, and to that very moment while locking up my bike to play in this game, believed my future was on the field at Dodger Stadium. Next thing I knew, Bob Eley, a kid with the thickest glasses I had ever seen and who already acted like an adult, was standing next to me. Bob was the league's official scorekeeper and announcer and had been invited to sit in on the meeting of the league's managers the night before as they voted on the all-star team that would get to travel to play in a tournament in Brawley, California, in August, in the desert near the Mexican border. The all-star team would stay with local families and play a week's worth of games. My friends and I lived for this kind of stuff, and I took it for granted that I would make the team.

Bob told me differently. "It was a close vote, but you did not make the team. Some of the managers wanted you, but others didn't." Several thoughts went through my head before I grabbed my gear and went over to the dugout:

- "That's not fair."
- "I deserved it."

- "How could Dale make it over me?"
- "I'm going to egg the houses of the managers that didn't vote for me!"

But the main thought I had was that I was not going to be an LA Dodger in the future. I wasn't completely devoid of reality by this time. I knew there was some merit in my not making the all-star team. But it still hurt. I also decided at that moment that I wasn't going to play baseball again. Though I didn't hold myself completely to that pledge and did play a couple more seasons, I never did it with the drive and commitment that I had before Bob Eley's news. I do know for a fact that I let go of my baseball dreams that day.

And, no, I didn't egg anybody's house either. Instead, I surprised myself by being as gracious as a fifteen-year-old could be. I congratulated my friends who made the team. I even traveled to Brawley with my mom, sat in the bleachers, and watched my friends play. It still didn't feel good, but I was trying to move on.

Then, a few weeks after that, some new grace did indeed come my way. The sports editor of our school newspaper decided to quit his position right before the start of school. Our school's baseball coach spoke to me privately and told me that I would be perfect for the job because I loved sports so much. Not only was I named sports editor, but I was also hired by the local daily newspaper to be a stringer reporter for our school's teams. By that time, I had turned sixteen and had my driver's license. The newspaper job paid $30 a week, which was more than enough for gas for my 1966 Mustang. I moved on from a baseball dream to a journalism dream. In one way or another, I have had the word "editor" by my job title ever since. God provided all of the graces for the head start.

PLAN FOR THE FUTURE

The baseball experience touched off a kind of pattern in my life: when I gave up something, God would often give me something new, different, and typically better. In the Catholic tradition, these experiences are sometimes known as "little deaths" and "little resurrections." Our lives are patterned on the Paschal Mystery of Christ's saving actions. Through Christ's Death, our death was destroyed, and through his Resurrection our life will be restored. The way to heaven, like the Way of the Cross, is not a straight or easy path. There are many questions, disappointments, and pains along the way. There are glimpses of perfection and the pure joy that awaits us in heaven too. God's grace helps us to persevere.

That's the way it was with the first disciples too. They were fishermen who left their boats to follow Jesus. The apostles James and John even seemed to abandon their father in the boat based on Jesus's obscure invitation to "come after me, and I will make you fishers of men" (Mt 4:19). It took the disciples some time before they understood who it was they were following and what would be expected of them as "fishers of men."

According to the gospel accounts, Jesus is very slow to reveal his exact identity. And even when Jesus does tell them that he will be rejected, suffer, and die, the disciples misunderstand how this relates to them, so he has to explain it clearly: "Whoever wishes to come after me must deny himself, take up his cross, and follow me. For whoever wishes to save his life will lose it, but whoever loses his life for my sake and that of the gospel will save it" (Mk 8:34–35).

Giving up youth baseball when it was probably the time was one thing, but getting married and giving up the life of a single person who was comfortable living alone in his one-bedroom apartment near the beach in Santa Monica was quite another. Being married is certainly a surrender of one's personal will and a blending of it with the will of another. I've discovered over the last thirty-seven-plus years that marriage to my wife Lisa trumps a millionfold going at life all alone. The reasons are many for this, but mainly the grace of the Sacrament of Matrimony has brought Christ into our lives in deeper ways. We have done our part to make each other more holy and to lead the other to the finish line in heaven. Lisa is much more "religious" now than she was when I first met her. She reads spiritual classics and participates fully in the Church's other sacraments. I hope these are things I have helped her with. For me, I have become more conciliatory, less reactive, and more cooperative due to learning these things from Lisa.

At our wedding, we chose the parable of the mustard seed for our gospel reading. The mustard seed is "the smallest of all the seeds, yet when full-grown it is the largest of plants" (Mt 13:32). We imagined our marriage like that. While we knew each other, we had never lived with each other. While we wanted to welcome children, we didn't know how many there would be or who they would be. While we wanted certain things in our careers, on our wedding day, Lisa was still in nursing school and I was a month away from transitioning from teaching to being a book editor. Needless to say, we didn't know how it was going to turn out in a lot of areas of life. We only knew that we were starting small and were hoping our lives would turn out full. We are at the time when we can review our lives and see how we did.

As much as I want to "do" things right up until Judgment Day, in our remaining years I really just want to appreciate living with my wife more. We won't have (as much) work, there are no school events to attend, and except for our youngest son, James, we have no adult children living with us at home. I now look out our kitchen window where two comfortable, reclining outdoor chairs have been on our back porch for years. I remember only a handful of times that Lisa and I sat next to each other on these chairs. I want to do more of that, and not just on Saturday evenings. We have a lot more to learn about each other and to appreciate how God has acted and is acting in our lives.

ACT IN THE PRESENT

One of the most important things we have already done to prepare to be saints is to be baptized. St. Irenaeus wrote that "Baptism is indeed the seal of eternal life" (CCC 1274). When Jesus gave the apostles his Great Commission to go out and create more disciples to the ends of the earth, he said clearly, "Whoever believes and is baptized will be saved; whoever does not believe will be condemned" (Mk 16:16).

Baptism is significant because this is when our character changed. Instead of sinful creatures marked with original sin, we became sons and daughters of God. We were given a spiritual mark that cannot be removed. This is a comforting thought to Catholic parents whose children have stopped practicing their faith for the time being.

Unfortunately, we forget what we or others in our name promised at our Baptism. We do renew our baptismal promises at Easter, but this can become perfunctory. Great saints have recommended that we renew our baptismal promises daily. St. Louis de Montfort said we should not only renew these vows daily but also place them in the hands of Mary so she can do the work of putting enmity between us and evil and helping us more fully recommit ourselves to her Son. For the present, we can renew and reflect on our baptismal promises every day. For example:

Do you reject Satan? And all his works? And all his empty promises? Satan, the prince of evil, is well out in the open these days and in the news. There are offenses against life, peace, freedom, and sexuality. It's easy to reject those things on a large scale. But how do we reject these attacks in our own personal lives? I want to be a spiritual warrior against Satan and his works by praying through Mary and watching his destruction. She has "crushed his head" already as predicted in Genesis 3:15. I want to enjoy watching our perfect, feminine Mother win the final battle and make sure that I remain on her side.

Do you believe in God, the Father, creator of heaven and earth? I need to remember each day that I am *created*. Everything has been a gift of a Creator, who is a Father. My own loving dad gave me so many good gifts from his entire person. Jesus asks, "How much more will the Father in heaven give the holy Spirit to those who ask him?" (Lk 11:13). We need to keep asking each day.

Do you believe in Jesus Christ, his only Son, our Lord, who was born of the Virgin Mary, was crucified, died, and was buried, rose from the dead, and is now seated at the right hand of the Father? The Incarnation is miraculous on the same scale as the Paschal Mystery. Christ performed the difficult work of suffering and dying for our sins, but the Incarnation—the eternal God coming into the world as one of us—made victory guaranteed.

Do you believe in the Holy Spirit, the holy catholic Church, the communion of saints, the forgiveness of sins, the resurrection of the body, and life everlasting? Without the gift of the Holy Spirit I would be lost and unable to believe any of these other things or to function in the world. When my own futile efforts fall short, my prayer when I face challenges is "Come, Holy Spirit." I appreciate Mary as the embodiment of the Holy Spirit and the direction she provides to maintain and increase my faith.

A lead engineer at Lockheed, Kelly Johnson, who designed a complex spy plane, is said to have come up with the acronym KISS: "Keep it simple, stupid." Because the planes were designed for battle, they had to be simple to maintain and be repaired by a pilot in the field, or they would not be effective and, in fact, useless. There is a parallel here with the way we practice our faith and go about trying to become saints. We might seek out advanced degrees in theology and lay prostrate on the floor for hours in prayer (neither bad things), but if we really want to keep it simple, we need to take our baptismal vows to heart, remember them, and put them into practice.

PRAY

Rejoice in the Lord always.
I shall say it again: rejoice!
Your kindness should be known to all.
The Lord is near.
Have no anxiety at all,

but in everything,
by prayer and petition,
with thanksgiving,
make your requests known to God.
Then the peace of God that surpasses all
understanding
will guard your hearts and minds in Christ
Jesus.

—Philippians 4:4–7

REFLECT

- Look at yourself through the eyes of God, your Creator. What are some things he loves about you? Don't be modest.

- What is a memory you have of a "little death" followed by a "little resurrection" that pointed you in a new direction?

- How can you remember and put into practice your baptismal vows on a daily basis?

CONCLUSION
While We Still Have Time

In grade school I wasn't the only one to stare at the clock that hung in the front of the room. The last twenty minutes before 3:10 dismissal seemed more like a month. Back then the minute hand on the clock would skip back a beat before it clicked ahead to the next minute. The millisecond it did that right before the bell rang was the longest one of all. We suffered through those last twenty minutes, waiting for school to end.

As we get older, we can't take any minute or millisecond for granted. We need to use all of the time we have left to the best of our capabilities. You can start by doing the things mentioned in this book, or create other experiences just like them, in order to live with greater faith, hope, and love as we prepare to meet Jesus face-to-face.

The irony is that though we must work out and prepare for our own salvation *in time*, in eternity, after our judgment, there will be *no time*. Remember, God doesn't give us two hundred or four hundred years; he gifts us with just enough time to freely choose to love him and our neighbor. If there was time in heaven, we might not want to go there.

But heaven is not like that. A heaven without time is one of those things our human minds are not built to completely comprehend. Archbishop Fulton J. Sheen pointed to some clues:

> Have you ever noticed that your happiest moments have come when eternity almost seemed to get inside your soul? When you are not conscious of time at

all. This is a hint of what heaven must be. It must be
outside of time, where you can possess all joys at one
and the same full moment.[1]

He named two moments as examples: a child's First Communion
and a couple's wedding. Both are occasions of love, with which
heaven will be filled.

You have probably had many days yourself when you can say
that "time flies." They are usually days that include happy events.
These are glimpses of heaven. I think of my annual reunions at
the Crest Lounge telling stories with my childhood friends and
especially our wedding reception held in the parish auditorium at St. Monica's Catholic Church when Lisa and I went table
to table greeting relatives, people we went to school with, and
parishioners. I can't believe how quickly these parties went from
start to finish. I wanted to talk with everyone and reminisce, but
time just ran out. There will be no time to run out of in heaven.

IT'S ONLY THE BEGINNING

The manager of the band Chicago, Peter Schivarelli, played football at Notre Dame in the 1960s. Because of this connection,
Chicago has played the halftime show at Notre Dame football
games three or four times since I have been on the field for
games. Each time, I sit on the team bench and listen to the horns
and sax and vocals of Chicago at a distance of about six feet.

I love it when the band plays their song "Beginnings" at that
close range. The long instrumental and the refrain repeated over
and over strikes me like a religious revival if I had ever been to
such a thing. They sing, several times over, that it is only the
beginning. It is true, earth life is only the very beginning of our
eternity. Will we even remember being here? Yes, we will. The
presence of our eternal souls and glorified bodies guarantees
that our identities and memories will persevere. But we will no
longer harbor any false caricatures of ourselves that we may have
created while living on earth when we reach heaven. We will
know ourselves in the authentic and sinless way God intended

for us to be. We will be known by family and friends and by God in ways we can't imagine. Our life today *is* only the beginning. I'm looking forward to heaven and all its surprises and am trying my best to prepare to get there while I still have time.

PRAY

> Lord of mercy,
>> you have made all things by your Word
>> and in your wisdom have gifted
>> humans with the freedom to choose you.
> Give me Wisdom
>> and do not reject me.
> For I am your servant,
>> and though someone weak and short-lived,
>> and lacking in comprehension of judgment,
>> and of laws,
>> I know that I desire you
>> and to be with you always.
> Have mercy on me.
> Bring me home to you.
> Amen.
>
> —based on Wisdom 9:1–6

APPENDIX

Ten More Catholic Experiences

There are unlimited ways to live a good Catholic life. Follow the same format as with the other experiences listed in this book. Remember how you have done something like it in the past. Plan for a deeper way you would like to do it in the future. Act in a simpler way to do it now. Don't forget to reflect on your experience and offer a prayer of thanks. Here are ten more ideas to get you started.

1. Run for Elected Office

Do you think you could make a difference as a member of your local school board or on a city commission? Gather a core team, and explore the way to get on the ballot. Alternatively, work on the campaign of someone you support. Another option is to run for parish council.

2. Create a Living Trust

Make sure all of your plans are in place for those who are left with your estate. Creating a trust is a loving thing to do. Your spouse, children, or other relative or friend will be able to grieve your death and celebrate your life if these worldly tasks are in order. In the same vein, make sure to plan your funeral and burial arrangements.

3. Become a Liturgical Minister

Parishes and dioceses offer training sessions to become a Eucharistic minister or lector. Many times the training sessions are held online and can be done at your convenience. A one-to-one interview with a parish staff member will help to determine how your personal gifts are suited to liturgical ministry.

4. Participate in a Nonliturgical Parish Ministry

There are several ministries to choose from and that correspond with your interests and skills. For example, bereavement ministers console others on any loss they have experienced—from the death of a relative to a divorce in the family. Homebound ministers run errands to the grocery store and pharmacy and sometimes do household chores for people who are unable to leave their homes. If you have teaching experience, train and become a catechist in the religious education program for children.

5. Support Expectant and New Mothers

Catholic-supported agencies for pregnant women and new mothers are in every diocese. One task is to partner one-to-one with an expectant mother and support her beyond the birth of her child. There are other general donation collections that are ongoing.

6. Care for the Environment

There are several organizations that take up the task of advo-cating for environmental responsibility and arranging for and participating in hands-on events to clean up parks, lakes, oceans, and forests.

7. Participate in a Secular Institute, Society of Apostolic Life, or Fraternal Organization

Secular institutes are a form of consecrated life for single lay-people (and diocesan priests). You would not profess religious vows or live in community but rather pray and work to aid the Church's task of evangelization. Societies of apostolic life are members who partner with religious communities but do not make public vows. An example of a Catholic fraternal organization for men is the Knights of Columbus.

8. Consecrate Yourself to St. Joseph

Mary will not be "jealous" if you consecrate yourself to her husband, St. Joseph. In fact, through the sharing of his virtues and his paternal care, St. Joseph will lead you to be even closer to Mary and Jesus.

9. Learn a Second Language

One suggestion is to brush up or learn some basic Spanish. A majority of newly arrived immigrants to the United States and to Catholic parishes are Spanish speaking. Help these new members of your community feel welcome. If you learn the language well enough, you might be able to help newly arrived people to prepare for US citizenship.

10. Make a Silent Retreat

A silent retreat is different than a directed retreat in which there is a scheduled program with speakers and presentations. Most retreat houses have silent retreats in which you read, meditate, and pray on your own while also being able to participate in the Divine Office and other liturgies held regularly.

NOTES

INTRODUCTION: GETTING READING FOR MY JUDGMENT DAY

1. "Bishop Fulton Sheen: The First "'Televangelist,'" *Time*, April 14, 1952, https://content.time.com/time/subscriber/printout/0,8816,857161,00.html.

2. "Fulton Sheen on the Last Four Things," Fulton J. Sheen Company, October 31, 2019, https://www.bishopsheen.com/blogs/news/fulton-sheen-on-the-last-4-things-love-is-the-key.

3. Joseph Pronechen, "Fulton Sheen on the 4 Last Things: Love Is the Key," *National Catholic Register*, October 31, 2019, https://www.ncregister.com/features/fulton-sheen-on-the-4-last-things-love-is-the-key.

4. Quotations from Archbishop Sheen are from "Fulton Sheen on the Last 4 Things: Love Is the Key," Fulton J. Sheen Company, Inc., October 31, 2019, https://www.bishopsheen.com/blogs/news/fulton-sheen-on-the-last-4-things-love-is-the-key.

5. Ignatius of Loyola, *The Spiritual Exercises of St. Ignatius of Loyola*, trans. Elder Mullan: (New York: P. J. Kennedy & Sons, 1914), 30.

6. Deborah Castellan Lubov, "We Must Memorize God's Beautiful Deeds in Our Lives," Catholic.net, April 22, 2016, https://catholic.net/op/articles/2430/cat/1243/we-must-memorize-gods-beautiful-deeds-in-our-lives-.html.

CHAPTER 2: PRAY REGULARLY

1. Ronda De Sola Chervin, *Quotable Saints* (Ann Arbor, MI: Servant Publications, 1992), 191.

2. Attributed to St. Teresa of Ávila.

3. Attributed to St. Thérèse of Lisieux.

4. Robert Hugh Benson, "In the Convent Chapel," in *The Light Invisible* (N.p.: Once and Future Books, 2005), 59.

5. "How to Recite the Chaplet," The Divine Mercy, accessed October 5, 2023, https://www.thedivinemercy.org/message/devotions/pray-the-chaplet.

CHAPTER 3: ATTEND DAILY MASS

1. Pope Francis, "General Audience," The Holy See, November 22, 2017, https://www.vatican.va/content/francesco/en/audiences/2017/documents/papa-francesco_20171122_udienza-generale.html.

2. Ronda De Sola Chervin, *Quotable Saints* (Ann Arbor, MI: Servant Publications, 1992), 79.

CHAPTER 4: STUDY SCRIPTURE

1. Attributed to St. Augustine.

2. Anugrah Kumar, "'I finished it!': Patricia Heaten celebrates reading entire Bible for the first time in her life," *Christian Post*, December 19, 2022, https://www.christianpost.com/news/patricia-heaton-reads-the-entire-bible.html.

CHAPTER 5: MAKE A PILGRIMAGE

1. Catholic News Agency, "The 70th miracle: Lourdes healing officially declared supernatural," February 12, 2018, https://www.catholicnewsagency.com/news/37743/the-70th-miracle-lourdes-healing-officially-declared-supernatural.

2. Catholic News Agency, "The 70th miracle: Lourdes healing officially declared supernatural."

3. Attributed to St. Bernadette Soubirous.

CHAPTER 6: SUPPORT THE POOR

1. Pope Francis, "Message of His Holiness Pope Francis for the Fifth World Day of the Poor," The Holy See, November 14, 2021, https://www.vatican.va/content/francesco/en/messages/poveri/documents/20210613-messaggio-v-giornatamondiale-poveri-2021.html.

2. Pope Francis, *Evangelii Gaudium* [The Joy of the Gospel], The Holy See, 2013, https://www.vatican.va/content/francesco/en/messages/poveri/documents/20210613-messaggio-v-giornatamondiale-poveri-2021.html.

3. Mother Teresa, *Words to Love By* (Notre Dame, IN: Ave Maria Press, 1983), 22.

CHAPTER 7: BUILD PHYSICAL FITNESS

1. Thomas John Paprocki, *Running for a Higher Purpose: 8 Steps to Spiritual and Physical Fitness* (Notre Dame, IN: Ave Maria Press, 2021), 62.

2. Peter Celano, *My Year with the Saints* (Brewster, MA: Paraclete Press, 2020), July 5 entry.

CHAPTER 9: STAY CONNECTED WITH FRIENDS

1. Attributed to St. John Bosco.

CHAPTER 11: CARE FOR THE SICK

1. Pope Francis, *Fratelli Tutti* [All Brothers], The Holy See, October 3, 2020, sec. 19.

CHAPTER 12: CHANGE YOUR LIFE

1. Pope Benedict XVI, "General Audience," The Holy See, September 3, 2008, https://www.vatican.va/content/benedict-xvi/en/audiences/2008/documents/hf_ben-xvi_aud_20080903.html.

CHAPTER 13: DRAW CLOSE TO THE BLESSED MOTHER

1. Jean-Pierre de Caussade, *Abandonment to Divine Providence: The Classic Text with a Spiritual Commentary by Dennis Billy, C.Ss.R.* (Notre Dame, IN: Ave Maria Press, 2010), bk. 1.

2. Jonathan Fleischmann, "Who Are You, O Immaculate Conception?" Saint Maximilian Kolbe, accessed October 24, 2023, https://saintmaximiliankolbe.com/who-are-you-o-immaculate-conception/.

3. Maximilian Kolbe, "Official Act of Consecration to Mary," Militia of the Immaculata, https://militiaoftheimmaculata.com/act-of-consecration-to-mary/.

4. Attributed to St. Louis de Monfort.

CHAPTER 14: PREPARE TO BE A SAINT

1. Stuart C. Devenish, *Ordinary Saints: Lessons in the Art of Giving Away Your Life* (Eugene, OR: Cascade Books, 2017), 384, quoting Thomas Merton, *The Seven Storey Mountain*.

CONCLUSION: WHILE WE STILL HAVE TIME

1. "Fulton Sheen on the Last 4 Things: Love is the Key," Fulton J. Sheen Company, Inc., October 31, 2019, https://www.bishopsheen.com/blogs/news/fulton-sheen-on-the-last-4-things-love-is-the-key.

Michael Amodei is executive editor and curriculum development manager at Ave Maria Press, where he writes and edits Catholic high school religion textbooks. He is the author of several books, including *Send Out Your Spirit, Catholic Essentials, The Ave Guide to the Scriptural Rosary,* and *The Ave Guide to Eucharistic Adoration.* Amodei also has acquired a number of spiritual books for Ave Maria Press, including *A Teen's Game Plan for Life* by Lou Holtz, *Holy Goals for Body and Soul* by Bishop Thomas Paprocki, and *Expect More!* by Muffet McGraw.

Amodei earned his bachelor's degree in English from Loyola Marymount University in Los Angeles, California, where he also earned a master's degree in religious education.

Amodei previously served as director of religious education and as a youth minister at St. Monica Catholic Church in Santa Monica, California. He also served as a math, religion, and gym teacher, as well as a Catholic Youth Organization sports coach at St. Monica Elementary School.

He is leader of the Ave Maria Press Chapter of Catholic Relief Services, a member of the Association of Catholic Publishers, and a third degree in the Knights of Columbus. Amodei has been a youth sports coach for more than forty years and is the field supervisor for home football games at the University of Notre Dame. Amodei lives with his family in South Bend, Indiana.